19.95

W9-AWQ-934

ELLA FITZGERALD

ELLA FITZGERALD

JAZZ
SINGER
SUPREME

CAROLYN WYMAN

An Impact biography

FRANKLIN WATTS
New York
Chicago
London
Toronto
Sydney

FOR

JAMES and VIOLA WYMAN,
who, instead of stopping
their daughter's music lessons
after she broke her rental clarinet,
chose to buy her an unbreakable,
plastic instrument.

Photographs copyright ©: Archive Photos, NYC: pp. 1, 3, 13 top; The Frank Diggs Collection: pp. 2, 6, 8, 9 top, 10, 11, 12 (both Popsie Randolph); New York Public Library, Schomburg Center for Research in Black Culture: pp. 4 top, 5 bottom; The Bettmann Archive: pp. 4 bottom, 5 top, 9 bottom; UPI/Bettmann Newsphotos: pp. 6, 14; Wide World Photos: pp. 13 bottom, 15, 16.

Library of Congress Cataloging-in-Publication Data

Wyman, Carolyn.
   Ella Fitzgerald : jazz singer supreme / Carolyn Wyman.
      p.   cm.—(Impact biography)
   Discography: p.
   Includes bibliographical references and index.
   Summary: Chronicles the personal life and singing career of the well-known jazz artist and discusses her impact on contemporary music.
   ISBN 0-531-13031-2
   1. Fitzgerald, Ella—Juvenile literature. 2. Singers—United States—Biography—Juvenile literature. [1. Fitzgerald, Ella. 2. Singers. 3. Jazz. 4. Afro-Americans—Biography.] I. Title.
ML3930.F5W9 1993
782.42165'092—dc20
[B]   92-41969 CIP MN AC

Contents

ACKNOWLEDGMENTS

The pleasure of studying a subject you love cannot be denied. Unfortunately, there was more to this book than just listening to Ella sing. For pointing me in the direction of invaluable information or for simply supplying that information I'd like to thank George Simon, Jack McKivigan, Pat Barnes, Frank Tirro, Vivian Perlis, Anna Zimmerman, Phoebe Jacobs, J. Richardson Dilworth, Ida Massenburg, Keter Betts, Patrice Pascual, William Halldin, Pat Hubbell, Harold Hornstein, Andrea Braverman, Kathleen Kudlinsky, Susan Purdy, Mary Jane Outwater, Johan Horne, Laurie Trotta, Lesley McCreath, Jr., and other members of the Yale University Class of 1935; Whitelaw Reid and other members of the Yale University Class of 1936; and the staffs of the Institute for Jazz Studies at Rutgers University, the Museum of Broadcasting, the Enoch Platt Free Library in Baltimore, Sterling Memorial Library at Yale University, the Music Division of the Lincoln Center Library for the Performing Arts, and the Schomburg Center for Research in Black Culture.

The International Women's Writing Guild deserves special thanks for providing the link to Franklin Watts and to two helpful and gracious editors there by the names of Reni Roxas and Victoria Mathews. I'm also indebted to Phil Greenvall for wise editorial and other advice.

Anyone who knows anything about modern personal computers will understand how grateful I am to Steve Griswold, Lee Bradley, and other members of the CCP/M User's Group for keeping my Kaypro alive through the writing of this book.

Thanks also to Kathy Katella, for encouragement that was my sword and shield during a time of many rejection slips.

Finally, I would like to thank Ella Fitzgerald for music that has brought me great joy.

CHAPTER ONE

A STAR IS BORN

Ella Fitzgerald stood backstage at the Harlem Opera House and hopped nervously from foot to foot. Earlier that day she and two girlfriends had drawn straws to determine who would perform at the Opera House's amateur contest. She had won the draw. But right now she didn't feel like a winner. She just felt very scared.

If an amateur hour audience didn't like a performer at some theaters in Harlem, a man dressed in a clown outfit would come out with a cap pistol and chase the performer off the stage. Ella imagined this happening to her, shivered, then peered out through an opening in the curtain to watch the two girls on stage. They were dancing and, judging from the applause, the audience seemed enthralled.

Ella had also been planning to dance—but now she didn't think it was such a great idea. These girls were really good. But before she could think about it, the announcer called her name. Ella stumbled onstage, her heart beating wildly. Somewhere through her fear, Ella heard the announcer tell the audience she was going to dance. The band struck up a tune. The announcer looked at her expectantly. But Ella could not do anything. Her legs felt like rubber; they wouldn't move the way she wanted.

Some people in the audience shifted impatiently in their seats; a few others began to chuckle. Ella wished she could run off the stage and all the way back to her home in Yonkers. Dancing in the streets or in her friends' backyards was one thing, but what made her think she was good enough to perform onstage in front of all these people?

Suddenly the announcer interrupted her thoughts.

"Well, if you're not going to dance you better do *something* up here," he said, sarcasm in his voice. That gave Ella an idea. If she couldn't control her legs well enough to dance, she would sing instead. She often sang along with the radio at home. Ella told the announcer the name of a tune by Connee Boswell, one of her favorite performers. Then she began to sing, quietly at first, but as the audience began to settle down and listen, louder and clearer.

When she finished, the audience not only applauded, they yelled for more. Ella looked at the announcer. He nodded yes. She launched into another song. Again, the crowd loved it. Again, they asked for more. Again, she sang.

Two songs later, Ella was awarded the $25 first prize, the equivalent of winning $250 today. It was only the first of hundreds of awards she has received in her career as one of the country's premier singers of jazz and popular music.

Ella's Harlem Opera House debut occurred in 1934, when Ella was probably fourteen years old. Although most sources say Ella was born on April 25, 1918, her longtime manager, Norman Granz, once said she was really born in 1920 but lied about her age when she was young in order to get around child labor laws that would have prevented her from singing.[1]

Although she was born in Newport News, Virginia, a big Navy and shipping port, Ella never knew anything about that city because she moved with her mother, Tempie, shortly after her father died. Since she was only an infant, she never remembered her father either, although her aunt told her that he liked to play guitar while her mother sang classical music.

Like millions of other southern blacks at the time, Ella's mother went north in search of work and affordable housing. Since Tempie had a sister, Virginia Williams, who lived in Yonkers, New York, about twenty minutes northeast of New York City, that's where she decided to move. Ella and her sister would spend a lot of time with their cousins and their aunt. There Ella and Tempie would also live with a man who would be like a stepfather to Ella.

Their neighborhood was poor but friendly. Tempie was part Indian, Ella's "stepfather" was Portuguese, and many of their neighbors were Italian and Spanish, but all the kids played together and all the adults helped one another out. "In the summer, everybody was up on the roof and we'd have block parties during the Italian festivals. It was all family. If a mother was going out, she'd throw her child in bed in somebody else's house," Ella later recalled.

Ella remembers only one incident of prejudice from those years. She was about eleven years old and a boy who was visiting from another neighborhood called her "nigger." In her anger, Ella pushed the boy and he fell down. "The other kids thought I had hit him—so I became a heroine at the school! They made him apologize, and after that everyone looked up to me, thought I was real bad," she said.[2]

Ella showed her spunky side one more time before her mother got it under control. Ella had appeared in a school play and she was walking down the street with her mother. Feeling superior because of how well she had performed in the play, she ignored a boy who came up to talk to her. Ella's mother gave her daughter a slap, then said, "Don't you ever go around where you don't speak to somebody, because someday that might be the very person who could be in a position to help you."

People especially needed help from one another then because America was in the middle of a great economic depression. The depression began in October of 1929, when the value of stocks in the United States declined to almost nothing. As a result, many thousands of banks, factories, and stores closed, leaving millions of Americans without jobs or money. With so many people out of work, competition for any job was stiff. Still, Ella's mother managed to find work as a caterer and at a laundry while her "stepfather" worked as a ditchdigger and a chauffeur. It was, Ella said later, "decent and respectable work. I'm proud of my mother. She always provided when she had to. She did her duty."[3] Still, the family was so poor that Ella always wore hand-me-down clothes, and her lunch was often only bread and a banana.

To help out, Ella took several odd jobs involving illegal activities (although she probably didn't understand at the time that they were illegal). At one point, for instance, she took numbers for New York's gangster-run lottery. She also once acted as lookout for the local house of prostitution. "I'd watch and knock on the door to let the girls know if the police were coming! Oh yes, I had a very interesting young life," Ella told a reporter after she had grown up.

Despite their money troubles, Ella's mother paid $5 (perhaps $25 in today's money) for a man to come every week and teach Ella how to play piano. The man had slit the skin between his fingers so that he'd be able to reach the piano keys better. Ella was so fascinated by this that she found it hard to concentrate on what he was trying to teach her. Because Ella made no progress and the lessons were expensive, Ella's mother stopped them.[4]

Ella also took music in school, but only in order to fulfill a requirement for an arts credit. "You had to take art or music, and I knew I was no artist," she remembered. She learned how to play harmonica and how to read music, but since she never really studied hard, she never excelled.

If Ella didn't study music seriously, she very much enjoyed listening to it. By 1927, there were two radio networks and Ella could hear the sound of musicians who played every night in Harlem right in her room. In addition, Ella's mother owned records by blues singer Mamie Smith, the Mills

Brothers, and other popular performers; she and Ella would often listen to them together.

Although black jazz musicians such as Duke Ellington, Louis Armstrong, and Fletcher Henderson were recording by this time, Ella was more interested in sentimental popular music. Ella especially liked a somewhat corny singer named Arthur Tracy who had a program on CBS radio, and Dolly Dawn, a soloist with George Hall's band. In fact, Ella would sometimes skip school to hear Dawn perform at a local theater.

But Ella's favorite singer was Connee Boswell. Boswell was a white woman from New Orleans who sang jazz-influenced tunes in close harmony with her two sisters. The Boswell Sisters had all played with the New Orleans Philharmonic Orchestra. Their classical training showed in the sophisticated musical arrangements they used. But Connee Boswell was a great admirer of Bessie Smith and Ethel Waters, and that showed in the way she used her voice. "She was actually my first singing teacher, but she never knew it," Ella later said of Boswell. "I met her through her 78 RPM recordings that I played over and over on my little phonograph."[5]

Ella also sang with the school glee club and in a local community chorus. But nobody made a big fuss about her voice the way they did about her dancing.

Although shy and gawky, Ella was a happy kid who enjoyed dancing with her friends. One of them remembers the dancing shows they used to put on in their backyards. Ella and her friends would also sometimes dance in the streets for money. She gained a reputation as being quite a good tap dancer. "Snakehips Ella," the kids called her, after Earl "Snakehips" Tucker, a particularly nimble dancer who performed in the Cotton Club Revue in Harlem. As a result, Ella began to think about a career as a professional dancer. Until then, the only thing Ella had ever thought about being was a doctor. She had even taken some Latin in school in preparation.

But this was not to be. Instead, one day Ella and two of her dancing friends dared one another to perform onstage at one of the amateur contests that were held in Harlem almost every day of the week. The girls decided to draw straws to determine who would compete in that next Wednesday's Harlem Opera House contest. Ella drew the smallest straw—and with it the support of her friends. "They believed I had talent; they gave me encouragement when I needed it. They forced me to do it," Ella has said.

Winning that contest was a turning point, not only because it changed her career ambition from dancer to singer, but because it made a poor, shy, gangly-looking girl feel wanted and loved in a way she never had before.

"Once up there I felt the acceptance, and love from the audience," she would later say. "I knew I wanted to sing for people the rest of my life."[6]

Coincidentally, that same evening another talented young amateur singer won the contest at the nearby Apollo Theater for her rendition of "In My Solitude." Her name was Pearl Bailey. In her autobiography, *The Raw Pearl,* she wrote, "I'm grateful I didn't go down the street to the Opera House. I doubt I would have made it there, for that night a young girl walked on stage, opened her mouth and the audience that had started out snickering ended up cheering."

Less than a year later, Ella quit school. In later life, she would be embarrassed about not knowing more about English grammar or how to read music without struggling, and would express regret for leaving school in the tenth grade. At that time, though, all she wanted to do was perform on the stage in Harlem.

CHAPTER TWO

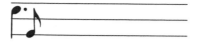

HARLEM HEYDAY

Harlem is that section of New York City bounded by Central Park on the south, 155th Street on the north, Morningside Drive on the west, and the East River. Until 1900, it was almost entirely a white neighborhood—and a rich one. But several changes in housing in Manhattan about the turn of the century turned that upside down. The construction of the new Pennsylvania railway station was forcing blacks to move from the West Side between 7th and 8th Avenues. Race riots in the other large black area, Hell's Kitchen, made people want to leave that neighborhood. At the same time, there was a surplus of housing in Harlem, a result of builders overestimating the number of whites who would want to commute from there to downtown on the newly constructed subway line. News of the beautiful new housing open to blacks reached as far south as Kentucky, the Carolinas, Georgia, and Virginia (where Ella came from) and attracted so many people that by 1920 much of Harlem was inhabited by blacks.

Among them were some of the nation's most talented black writers and artists. Working together, they created a new movement in the arts known as the Harlem Renaissance. Entertainers were also part of the Renaissance, and theaters and clubs sprang up all over the area to spotlight their talents. Clubs featured the big bands of Duke Ellington and Fletcher Henderson, and vaudeville shows featured entertainers such as Ethel Waters, Bill "Bojangles" Robinson, and choruses of dancing girls.

Although the entertainers were black, many of the patrons were whites from other parts of Manhattan drawn by the talent and the chance to drink undisturbed. In 1917, the U.S. Congress had approved a new amendment to the Constitution that prohibited the manufacture, sale, and transportation of alcoholic beverages. The groups that had pushed for the passage of the so-called Prohibition amendment argued that drinking damaged people's health and promoted bad behavior and poverty. The amendment was ratified in 1919, and after it went into effect in 1920, it was illegal to buy or sell liquor in this country. But many places continued to sell liquor illegally to the people who ignored the national ban on drinking. Among the customers were the New York City elite; most poor people could not afford the high prices charged for liquor by the illegal bootleggers. In New York City, a large number of the illegal bars, called speakeasys, were located in Harlem.

But whites didn't go to Harlem just to drink. By

this time, black musical shows that had originated in Harlem were drawing record crowds on Broadway, and it became fashionable among high society to travel from other parts of Manhattan to Harlem to discover the talent there before anyone else. In fact, some of the biggest and best clubs these celebrities and sophisticates patronized (the Cotton Club and Connie's Inn, for example) didn't allow blacks to attend.

This racial segregation was sanctioned by laws that had been put in place in the United States from 1890 on. Although blacks ostensibly gained full citizenship and the right to vote with the passage of the Fourteenth and Fifteenth Amendments to the Constitution after the end of the Civil War, many southern states quickly passed local laws (called Jim Crow laws, after the name of a black character in an old song) that placed restrictions on voting rights and called for the segregation of blacks and whites. Jim Crow laws in certain states required whites and blacks to use separate telephone booths, rest rooms, building entrances, hotels, and even different Bibles in court to swear oaths. The spread of these laws was upheld by a U.S. Supreme Court decision in the case of *Plessy v. Ferguson* in 1896. That decision supported the state of Louisiana's right to require blacks to use separate facilities on railroad cars as long as they were equal to those provided for whites. That "separate but equal" rule was used to justify segregation in all kinds of other public settings, including public schools. In point of fact, though, separate was rarely equal. Black schools in the South in 1916, to give one example, had higher pupil-to-teacher ratios, shorter calendar years, and much less money to spend than white ones.

Seven hundred thousand blacks migrated to northern cities between 1890 and 1920 and another 700,000 between 1920 and 1930, in part to escape the South's segregation. What they found in the North was a subtler form of racism, enforced by custom rather than law, that made it almost impossible to find high-paying industrial jobs, or housing anywhere but in overcrowded, segregated slums that were breeding grounds for illness and crime. But visitors never saw the residential slums of Harlem; to them, Harlem was a playland, a glamorous and vital place to drink and be entertained by America's premier black entertainers.

Before she even thought of performing herself, Ella and her friends used to take the train to Harlem to see shows at some of the clubs and to get the autographs of their favorite stars, people such as singer Billie Holiday and bandleader Chick Webb. It was winter when she got Webb's and, Ella remembers, "It was freezing cold, but he signed that autograph for me."[1]

In addition to professional entertainment, most of the clubs sponsored amateur contests for aspiring hopefuls. At the time Ella won the contest at the Harlem Opera House in 1934, an amateur singer or dancer could compete in contests in Harlem three or four nights a week. After winning that first contest, Ella went back to compete as often as she could.

Although Ella had skinny legs, wore ill-fitting clothes, and seemed nervous on stage, she had a beautiful, clear voice and a fresh and innocent stage manner audiences liked. She won several more contests, including one at the Apollo Theatre, a place known for having some of the most skeptical audiences in the city. Saxophonist Benny Carter was at one of these shows, and was so impressed by Ella's talent that he arranged for her to audition for bandleader Fletcher Henderson, who was looking for a new vocalist. John Hammond, a record producer who had helped advance the careers of such great jazz artists as Count Basie and Billie Holiday, was invited to come along. Ella went to Henderson's house, sang her Connee Boswell songs for the two men, and waited expectantly. But all Henderson said was, "Don't call me, I'll call you."

"I thought she was nice," Hammond would say later. "She had this lovely, smooth, silky voice. But for me, she didn't have any of the excitement and sex Billie Holiday had."[2]

Not long afterward, word of Ella's vocal gifts reached officials at CBS Radio. Ella won an audition to appear on the radio show hosted by her old idol, Arthur Tracy, and contracts were drawn up promising her a career buildup to rival Connee Boswell's. Ella was ecstatic.

But then, less than two weeks later, Ella's mother and cousin took a neighborhood boy out for a drive in their car and had an accident. As Ella understands it, "Mother grabbed the boy to protect him and struck her head on an iron bar. The injury never healed inside and she died not too long afterwards."[3] This left Ella orphaned and a minor, with nobody to sign the radio contract for her. The deal was off.

At first, Ella lived with her aunt, Virginia Williams. Then social workers for the state of New York sent Ella to the Riverdale Orphanage in Yonkers, where, among other things, she learned how to type and take dictation. She must have learned her lessons well because years later, when she took part in a speedwriting competition after delivering a commencement speech at the Buchanan Business Institute, Ella placed second, doing 290 words in four minutes.

Not one to talk a lot about her personal life and especially about her troubles, Ella has said very little publicly about this time. But it was about then that Ella lost an amateur show for the first time. Wearing a black mourning dress and looking forlorn, Ella walked onstage at the Lafayette Theater and began to sing "Lost in a Fog." She soon realized that the pianist didn't know the right chords to the song and, in trying to follow him, she soon lost her place. The audience began booing and Ella ran off the stage in tears.

In the years since, Ella has performed at thousands of concerts, jazz festivals, and clubs to the enthusiastic acclaim of millions of fans. And yet the memory of that night at the Lafayette has stayed with her. For years afterward, she would burst into tears at the slightest criticism, and after a concert would ask complete strangers if she had done okay.

Fortunately, her experience at the Lafayette did not keep her from entering more amateur contests. "People always assume you got a lucky break, but it isn't where you come from, it's where you're going that counts, and how your attitude is, and not getting discouraged," she has explained. Returning to the amateur hour at the Harlem Opera House in February 1935, she won the first prize: a week-long engagement with Tiny Bradshaw's band for $50.

"They put me on right at the end, when everybody had their coats on and was getting ready to leave. Tiny said, 'Ladies and gentlemen, here is the young girl who's been winning all the contests,' and they all came back and took their coats off and sat down again.''[4]

It was either at this performance or another about the same time that Ella was spotted by Bardu Ali, an announcer with Chick Webb's band. Like Benny Carter, Ali was impressed by Ella's talents and recommended her to his boss. But Webb's band was known for its instrumental and dance music, not for slower ballads that might be sung by a vocalist. Moreover, the band already had a singer (his name was Charlie Linton), and Webb saw no need for another.

One day a couple of weeks after Ella's engagement with the Bradshaw band, Ali was at the Apollo Theatre between shows and spotted Ella hanging around backstage. She was wearing her usual hand-me-down clothes, including boys' shoes, and eating a hot dog. Knowing that Webb wouldn't agree to an audition if he was asked, Ali snuck Ella into Webb's dressing room while the band was onstage. When Webb returned for intermission, Ali locked the door of the dressing room and forced him to sit down and listen to Ella sing her Connee Boswell songs ("Judy," "Believe It Beloved," and "The Object of My Affection"). Webb admitted that she sounded terrific, called up the band manager, Moe Gale, and asked him to come over to meet Ella.

Gale got one look at Ella and her clothes and said, "You're kidding." Later Gale recalled, "She looked incredible. Her hair disheveled, her clothes just terrible."

"Don't look at her, listen to the voice," said Webb.[5] He did, and was also impressed. With Gale's approval, Webb agreed to take Ella to a dance they were scheduled to play at Yale University the next night. If the college kids liked her, Webb said, he would give her a job with his band.

CHAPTER THREE

AUDITIONING

The man Ella sneaked into a dressing room to meet was one of the most talented drummers and bandleaders in Harlem. From all accounts, Chick Webb was also a nice person—the type of boss who would rehire a musician even though he had left the band without any warning, or pay a musician who was sick his regular salary even though he couldn't work.

Perhaps Webb was so sensitive to the problems of others because he had some major ones of his own. As a very little boy, Webb had fallen down a flight of stairs and injured his spine. A case of tuberculosis he contracted a few years later complicated the injury, causing him to grow up hunchbacked, unusually short (as an adult he was little more than four feet tall), and with partially paralyzed legs. In fact, Webb was given the name Chick because he looked as tiny and frail as a young bird. But Webb didn't act like an invalid or feel sorry for himself. Instead, he was a witty and outgoing kid who was always at the center of the liveliest crowd.

When one of his doctors suggested drumming as a way for Webb to exercise his stiffened limbs, Webb got drumsticks and began to bang on every pot and pan around the house and every trash can or fencepost he passed in his walks around his native city of Baltimore. At the age of nine, he took a job selling newspapers to earn enough money to buy a drum set. With his selling skills (he once boasted of selling 3,000 papers in a single day), he soon had his drum set. He had a special extension put on the pedal so he could reach the bass drum.

The drive and determination that Webb showed in overcoming his handicap showed in his style of playing: Although his weak limbs didn't allow him to play loudly or with great precision, "he could propel such a drive, simply by beating such great time and exploding at just the right moments, that . . . he would charge the atmosphere of anywhere he played," big band historian George Simon has written.

In 1924, at only sixteen years of age, Webb moved to New York City with a guitarist friend, John Trueheart. There Webb met Duke Ellington, fast becoming one of the most respected and well-connected musicians in town. Ellington was so impressed with the young drummer that he got Webb a job leading a quintet at a club called the Black Bottom. Webb had never led a group before, but Ellington told him it was easy. "All you do is collect the money," he said.

A year later, Webb began playing at the Paddock Club with seven other musicians. Over a period of years, this group grew to big band size and included some of the most talented musicians in Harlem. At one time or another, Benny Carter, Johnny Hodges, Edgar Sampson, and Taft Jordon all played with Webb, helping to create the driving sound that made his band among the most popular with dancers.

Nevertheless, Webb and his musicians did not make a great deal of money. In part, this was because other bandleaders recognized Webb's talent at finding good musicians and kept hiring men away from him. So Webb had trouble keeping his band together. It also was because of the segregation that created separate clubs, radio stations, and record labels for black and white musicians. The white majority of the population heard mainly white musicians when they listened to the radio or records, and so tended to prefer them. Even though black singers such as Billie Holiday and Bessie Smith had recordings, white stars such as Bing Crosby, Guy Lombardo, and Kate Smith had the biggest hits and made the most money.

In fact, many of the songs Webb saxophonist Edgar Sampson wrote, and the Webb band performed, songs such as "Don't Be That Way," "If Dreams Come True," and "Stompin' at the Savoy," only became famous when white clarinetist Benny Goodman played them. However, as the first popular white jazz musician to hire blacks to work with his band, Goodman was also responsible for helping whites to appreciate just how important blacks' contributions were to the music.

In fact, jazz was the creation of black musicians who lived in New Orleans in the early 1900s. Although the exact origins of jazz are unclear, most people believe it evolved from blues, spirituals, gospel, work songs, African rhythms, folk songs, marches, and ragtime—all different types of music being played by blacks at the turn of the century. Then as now, jazz is defined by such unique characteristics as improvisation (music that is "made up" on the spot rather than memorized or written down), blues (slightly flatted notes), and syncopation (music played on an off-beat). The result was music considerably freer and more full of feeling than what most Americans had heard before. For this reason—and also probably because it was created by a minority group long oppressed and discriminated against—mainstream America initially frowned on jazz. At first, much of the music that came to be known as jazz was played at black funerals or parades by small bands. But before long, the playing of it was relegated to bars in unsavory neighborhoods that "nice" folks didn't venture near.

Between 1910 and 1920, many jazz musicians moved out of the South to such cities as Chicago, Kansas City, and New York. In each of these places, the music evolved into slightly different forms.

Jazz became so popular during the 1920s that the period became known as the Jazz Age. In New York in particular, it became all the rage to dance to the lively ragtime piano music of Fats Waller and Jelly Roll Morton. Young women dancers of the day who wore short skirts and long pearl necklaces and danced and drank the nights away were known as flappers. But by the beginning of the next decade, the stock market crash and the economic depression that followed made both the music and all the fun the flappers were having seem frivolous. Instead, audiences demanded sentimental songs and more sedate, formally arranged music played by dance bands led by Paul Whiteman, Duke Ellington, Don Redman, and Fletcher Henderson.

It was only after Franklin D. Roosevelt became president in 1932 and began to enact policies that helped ease people's money problems that jazz became lively again. Because of its emphasis on rhythm, this new style of jazz was known as swing. And it was perfectly suited for dancing.

By the time Ella was preparing for her audition at Yale, every radio station and every ballroom in Harlem featured swing music. The different bands—and there were hundreds of them—distinguished themselves by the unique way their music was arranged (distributed among the various sections of the orchestra) and the skill the band members displayed in their solo improvisations. Young people from all walks of life, including those at prestigious universities like Yale, followed the bands and their players as closely as they followed major league baseball.

Because Yale is located only a short train ride from New York City, students visited Harlem on weekends to hear firsthand some of the musicians they had heard on the radios in their dorm rooms. Some of the wealthiest students—and there were many wealthy students at Yale—could even afford to bring a pianist such as Art Tatum or Erroll Garner to New Haven to perform for parties in their dorm rooms. More commonly, a group of students would pool their money to hire a group to play for their proms and fraternity parties.[1]

Yale was an all-male school then, so on prom weekends the students' dates usually came from out of town on Friday night and stayed in special, chaperoned accommodations through Sunday night. It was a whole weekend of nearly nonstop partying. In March of 1935, the boys of St. Elmoe Hall dormitory pooled their money to hire the Chick Webb band to entertain at one of a half-dozen parties held the night after the prom.[2]

Meanwhile, in New York City, some members of the Webb band had pooled their money to take Ella to a beauty parlor and buy her some makeup. Ella could get away with her gawky appearance at an amateur hour, but the Yale gig was a real job. It could be her last real job unless she made the grade.

It's not hard to imagine how nervous Ella must have been when she climbed onto the band bus in the gown Tiny Bradshaw and his chorus girls had bought for her when she had worked with them. Seeing the elegant homes in the Connecticut suburbs and the regal, ivy-covered stone buildings at Yale, Ella felt that she had entered a different world. The Webb band set up to play at the end of a long, wood-paneled room in the St. Elmoe dorm building. By 8 P.M., the place was packed with Yale students and their dates—most of them dressed better than Ella was. How could they possibly like me—I'm so different from them, Ella probably thought as she sat in a chair toward the back of the band, waiting.

Finally, Ali Bardu beckoned Ella onstage. As she shyly stepped up to the microphone, the crowd quieted. Guys put their arms around their girls as they listened to Ella sing. When she had finished, they cheered and applauded as enthusiastically as any Harlem audience. Ella launched into her second song. As she finished her third, the students crowded around the bandstand, yelling, "We want to hear the girl sing." As they did, that warm feeling, that feeling of being accepted that Ella craved, came over her in waves. When the dance was over, Webb came up to her and told her what the applause had led her to suspect: in a week, she would be singing at the Savoy!

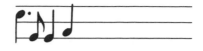

CHAPTER FOUR

UNDER WEBB'S WING

Although the New Haven college kids reacted enthusiastically to Ella's singing, the real test would be when she sang in the clubs and ballrooms of Harlem. That was where swing swang the most. And the swingingest of all the clubs was the Savoy.

Located on the second floor of a building that took up most of the block at 140th Street and Lenox Avenue, the Savoy was twice as wide as it was deep, with two bandstands, a disappearing rear stage, and an oval, racetrack-like dance floor that gave it the nickname "The Track." The floor was the biggest in Harlem. Because of this, its reputation for safety, and its open-door policy to people of all races, the Savoy attracted some of the biggest crowds and best dancers. Some would stay until six o'clock in the morning.

Popular dances of the day included the Jitterbug, the Congeroo, and the Suzy Q. But the most popular dance of all was the Lindy Hop, named after Charles Lindbergh, the aviator who made the first solo trans-Atlantic flight in 1927. The movements of the dance (a male dancer tossed his partner in the air, then slid her along the floor and through his legs) imitated a plane's takeoff and landing.

A band that couldn't get people onto the floor was not invited back to the Savoy. Really swinging bands such as Webb's could get everyone dancing in such a frenzy that the floor of the ballroom would literally bounce up and down. In 1934, Edgar Sampson wrote a hit song about the place called "Stompin' at the Savoy." A twenty-minute version of the song "Stardust," which built to a frenzy as the whole band joined in with maracas, claves, and other percussion instruments, was another of the band's specialties.

Before Webb could fulfill his promise to Ella and let her join in all the excitement on the Savoy bandstand, he had to solve one problem. Ella was a fifteen-year-old orphan and, as she had discovered when she had been asked to sing on Arthur Tracy's radio show, New York City labor laws wouldn't allow a minor to work without the permission of a legal guardian. Webb, then twenty-six, and his wife, Sallye, talked it over and decided to adopt Ella legally, giving her a home, a job, and more confidence in her singing abilities. "I always thought my music was pretty much hollering. He didn't," Ella would later say.

But Webb did think Ella needed to forget Connee Boswell and forge her own vocal style. To help her do that, Webb coached her in singing technique and bandstand manners. "Always sing with the beat!" he told her. He also demonstrated

how she should sit, stand, and acknowledge applause while onstage.

Webb introduced Ella to the Savoy crowd
gradually, at first only allowing her to sing the
chorus on an occasional up-tempo number. He
didn't think she was ready for the slower ballads.
"You never want to be someone who goes up
fast, because you come down the same way. And
you meet the same people coming down as you
do going up," Webb explained.

Sometimes Ella got impatient. Once, when
Webb let the male vocalist, Charlie Linton, sing a
ballad originally planned for her, Ella burst into
tears on the bandstand. But usually she loved
working. When she wasn't singing, jazz historian
George T. Simon remembers, "She would usually
stand at the side of the band, and as the sections
blew their ensemble phrases, she'd be up there
singing along with all of them, often gesturing
with her hands as though she were leading the
band." Other times she would Lindy Hop with the
dancers or other performers such as singer Joe
Williams.

The Savoy crowd took an immediate liking to
Ella. She was about their age and so perhaps
they identified with her and understood her nervousness. Her voice was fresh and wholesome,
her delivery simple, and she had a sure sense of
rhythm as well as an ability to communicate
warmth and joy through the music. One man who
used to hang out at the Savoy with his friends
when he was in high school remembers the first
night he heard Ella sing at the Savoy. "One night
Chick Webb comes over and says, 'Hey, Peter, I
want you to meet a little girl. And I want you to
hear this girl sing.' And he trotted out a very fright-

ened and nervous youngster wearing a gingham dress and with a flower in her hair," said Peter Dean. "We went nuts for her. We all loved her. . . . [From] the beginning she sang with all that freedom and all that excitement."

Pianist and arranger Mary Lou Williams remembers hearing Ella at the Savoy at about the same time. "I heard a voice that sent chills up my spine . . . I almost ran to the bandstand to find out who belonged to the voice, and saw a pleasant-looking, brown-skinned girl, standing modestly and singing the greatest."

Before long, Ella's fans at the Savoy were joined by the thousands who heard her featured on late-night radio broadcasts from the club. Her growing fame forced Webb to include her in a recording session for Decca. The song was called "Love and Kisses," and shortly after it was released Ella and the band traveled to Philadelphia for a concert. After the concert, the group went to a restaurant with a jukebox that featured their new song. But because the jukebox was in a bar area, and Ella was underage, she was not allowed to enter. "So I had some fellow who was over twenty-one go in and put a nickel in while I stood outside and listened to my own voice coming out," Ella recalled.[1]

Despite this heady experience, Ella continued to act just like any other teenager. Arriving at a new town while traveling with the band, "I'd get out of the bus and the first thing I wanted to do was play baseball." At one point she took up the accordion, but it was too heavy for her to carry "and the fellows in the band got tired of lugging it around, so that was the end of that," Ella said.

Although Ella found ways to have fun, many

musicians who traveled with big bands in those days found it difficult and grueling. Because planes and trains were too expensive, most groups traveled in cars or buses, which weren't as comfortable as they are today. Many times the group would arrive at the ballroom just before the job, change in the bathrooms, play, eat some sandwiches that had been brought backstage, then climb back in the bus and sleep while riding—often hundreds of miles—to the next job. Even when they did have time to stop at a restaurant or stay in a hotel, black bands traveling in the South could have trouble finding places that would do business with them. Webb trumpet player Taft Jordon recalled, "You'd play towns where you'd have four or five thousand people there [at the concert], and you couldn't find a place to eat. One time in Columbia, Tennessee, [we] had to go to the back of the place [to get served food] then the police came along and made 'em stop."[2]

Even famous performers such as Louis Armstrong were not spared such treatment. He once recalled, "When I was coming along, a black man had hell. On the road he couldn't find no decent place to eat, sleep or use the toilet—service station cats see a bus of colored bandsmen drive up and they would spring to lock their restroom doors."

Pops Foster, a bassist who played with Armstrong in New Orleans and elsewhere, said, "If you had a colored bus driver back then, they'd lock him up in every little country town for 'speeding.' It was very rough finding a place to sleep in the South. You couldn't get into the hotels for whites and the colored didn't have any hotels.

You rented places in private homes, boarding houses, and whorehouses."

If a band was integrated, then black and white members almost always had to stay in different places. Trumpeter John Best recalled a night when he, drummer Zutty Singleton, and singer Billie Holiday were stopping in West Virginia as members of the Artie Shaw Band.

"When we reached Parkersburg, Zutty asked to be let out at a black hotel and suggested to Billie that she get out there too, as they were 'down South' and couldn't stay at the 'white only' hotel downtown. However, Billie was determined to find this out for herself. She found out, the hard way, and was told that there were no rooms available. I had to take her back to the place where Zutty had checked in and in the meantime he had [gotten] the only room with a private bath."

To avoid these problems, black entertainers such as Duke Ellington, Cab Calloway, and Bessie Smith traveled by train, renting their own private Pullman sleeping and dining cars. But that didn't protect them from what happened when they reached the dancehalls where they were supposed to play.

Former Calloway band member Milt Hinton recalled a dance the group played for a bunch of Longview, Texas, cowboys. ". . . the prejudice was terrible. Some of [the audience members] would say, 'I'd pay a three-hundred-dollar fine just to hit one of those boys.' . . . The promoter . . . would put us in a room to keep the people from getting to us. The dance would always end up in a fight. When they didn't see us they'd fight amongst themselves. I can tell you I was scared."

The guys in the band probably shielded Ella from many of these indignities. If Webb was Ella's adoptive father, the members of the band treated her like a younger sister, calling her "Sis" and trying to keep their language clean in her presence. Dizzy Gillespie, who toured with Ella a few years later, noted how Ella "always played the role of the lady." Journalists have often commented on the formality of Ella's speech. She almost always precedes names with titles such as Miss or "the late" and once she said she wished other people would call her Miss Fitzgerald instead of Ella.

The Webb band, like its leader, had always been congenial. Taft Jordan had an infectious grin and could do a great Louis Armstrong imitation. Sax player and composer Edgar Sampson was the group's spokesman. His friendly relations with music journalists and gentle handling of pesky fans earned him the nickname "The Lamb." Band members were always joking around, and Ella's lackluster interest in her appearance was a favorite target of their kidding. Edgar Sampson remembered, "It would be 'Hey, Sis, where'd you get those clothes?' . . . And, 'Sis, what's with the hairdo?' But Ella always took it in good spirits." Her good spirits seemed contagious for, after Ella joined the band, historian Simon noted, "the whole spirit of the band pick[ed] up perceptibly."

Another thing that got the guys going was a good battle with another band. Because the Savoy had two bandstands, club management always hired bands to perform alternate sets (on Saturdays, one would play from 8:30 to 9:30 P.M.; the other from 9:30 to 10:30 and so on until 6 A.M. Sunday morning). It soon became a tradition for bands visiting the club to challenge the house band to a battle of musicianship, the winner to be determined by audience applause. Webb enjoyed the challenge of these battles and used his head, as well as his drumming hands, to win them. One of his strategies was to let the visiting band play all their best numbers and then, after they were tired, begin playing the best he could. In fact, Webb got the job at the Savoy after club management saw him defeat the bands of Fletcher Henderson and King Oliver. He had also triumphed over the Casa Loma Orchestra and Erskine Hawkins.

But Webb's most famous battle was waged against the Benny Goodman band on May 11, 1937. Goodman had been dubbed "the King of Swing" and led the most popular swing band then playing. But he was a white man playing a type of music created by blacks—and he had never played a concert head to head with a black band in Harlem. However, Goodman often stopped by the Harlem clubs to listen and learn. One day not long before the Webb battle, Goodman went to the Savoy hoping to hear the Webb band and get some ideas as to what songs he could play to beat them. But when Webb spotted Goodman in the audience, he slowed down the tempo on all the songs to fool Goodman into thinking his band did not swing as much as it really did.

The night of the battle, mounted police and fire department reserves were called in to control the crowds gathered in and around the Savoy. Four thousand people crammed inside the club, so many that there was no room to dance. Another 5,000 outside had to be turned away. The

Goodman band played the first number, a song called "Peckin'," and the crowd roared its approval. But when Webb replied with an opening volley on his drums, the crowd screamed, yelled, and whistled crazily.

For five hours the music went on, the bands alternating back and forth, the music continuing to get louder and hotter. By the time Webb and his orchestra played a song called "Harlem Congo," Webb was grinning. It was clear that the crowd was in his favor. When Ella got up to the microphone to begin singing, the crowd locked arms and swayed back and forth in time to the music. Webb finished the evening with a drum solo that received a thunderous ovation. Goodman and his drummer, Gene Krupa, stood in awe. "I'll never forget that night," Krupa said later. "He just cut me to ribbons—made me feel awfully small."

Later pianist Benny Payne explained how easily Webb had been able to defeat Goodman. According to Payne, Webb actually had three sets of music he used when battling other bands. "The third was mild stuff, number two was hot stuff, and number one would blow you away. Chick used his number three book on Benny Goodman; he and his band didn't even work up a sweat."

The next year, Webb faced his next logical rival: Count Basie. Once again, the place was packed, with the crowd including many musicians who hurried uptown after Benny Goodman's concert at Carnegie Hall earlier that evening. But this time the audience rooted for Basie. Basie saxophonist Lester Young had a "sound [that] was strange and enticing. Billie Holiday and Jimmy

Rushing sang their songs, and Basie led a rhythm section which even Webb could not beat," jazz writer Stanley Dance later recalled.

Webb also once lost to Duke Ellington, and legend has it that "the Duke" and his musicians played so hard and loud during that battle that several of the club's windows popped![3]

Even in contests that Webb did not win, newspaper accounts singled out Ella as being one of the band's primary assets. At the beginning of 1937, readers of the jazz magazine *Down Beat* confirmed that opinion by voting her best female vocalist. At about this time, Ella made a string of successful recordings for Decca, including "I'll Chase the Blues Away," "Swing Me a Swing Song and Let Me Dance," "A Little Bit Later On," "T'ain't What You Do, It's the Way That You Do It" and "If You Can't Sing It, You'll Have to Swing It," which became better known by the title, "Mr. Paganini."

This was at a time when singers—especially female band singers—were not held in the highest esteem. Most band leaders considered their female singers to be mere window dressing, something for male members of the audience to look at and admire. The women also came in handy when the band members needed a few moments of playing easy accompaniment after a particularly difficult song.

Many of these women did not really understand jazz or know how to swing at all. Ella and Billie Holiday were two wonderful exceptions. Ella was born with many of the assets that make her a great jazz singer, including an innate sense of what's in tune and what isn't, her wide-ranging voice, and a feeling for rhythm. But her precise diction and exquisite phrasing were probably learned by listening to the musicians in the band. "I've always felt that where I got my education was with the musicians . . . I've always been fortunate enough to have the kind of musicians who let me know if I'm singing or just skating . . . If the musicians like what I do, then I feel I'm really singing."

But Ella did more than merely absorb the music being played around her. She sought out opportunities to work at her craft. After concerts, she would gather with the other musicians to jam or play informally. Guitarist Barney Kessel remembers once having breakfast with Ella, Lester Young, and his wife. "While we waited to give our breakfast order I pulled out my guitar and she and Lester started making up fabulous things on the blues.

"Another time, when we were touring Switzerland, instead of gossiping with the rest of the troupe on the bus, she and I would get together and she'd take some tune like 'Blue Lou' and sing it every way in the world. She'd do it like Mahalia Jackson and like Sarah [Vaughan] and finally make up new lyrics for it. She would try to exhaust every possibility . . ."[4]

Ella's skill and professionalism helped define the heights jazz singing could reach, thereby making it easier for women singers who came after her to be seen not as just pretty faces but as musicians on an equal level with the instrumentalists in the band.

Even the defeated Benny Goodman recognized Ella's talents, asking her to sit in on a recording session and sing lead vocals on "Take Another Guess," "Did You Mean It?," and

"Goodnight, My Love." (When Decca, the recording company that had Webb under contract, heard about it, they forced R.C.A. Victor to recall the three songs, all collector's items today.) Goodman also expressed interest in hiring her for his band. So did Jimmy Lunceford, who offered her $75 a week.

When Ella first started singing for Webb he had paid her $12.50 a week. She was now making $50. But as she explained later, "I would never have left that band. It was like my family." In gratitude for her loyalty, Webb raised her salary to $125 a week—a fortune during a time when most people made about $35.

The raise was also a symbol of a bigger change. Recognizing Ella's enormous talent and seeing how the public responded to it, Webb began tailoring his band's performances more and more to her, letting some of the band's instrumental strengths wane. Some critics complained that the band itself had deteriorated, playing commercial clichés and childish pop tunes, and that it was no longer really playing jazz.

A look at some of the titles of the songs Ella recorded with the band during this period illustrates the point. They included the novelty number "Got A Pebble in My Shoe" and the Yiddish tune "Bei Mir Bist Du Schoen." But silly songs were all that people seemed to want to hear in 1938. "The Dipsy Doodle," "The Flat Foot Floogie with the Floy Floy," and "My Wubba Dolly" were all bestsellers. A singer named Maxine Sullivan even had a hit jazzing up the old Scottish folk song "Loch Lomond." But none of these captured the public's imagination as much as the novelty song Ella wrote that spring.

Ella and the Webb band were playing at a restaurant in Boston, when Webb, not feeling well, checked into a hospital. During a band rehearsal, Ella began fooling around at the piano with the idea of writing a song for Webb. She and Webb had written a song together the year before ("You Showed Me the Way") that was good enough to have been recorded by Billie Holiday. As she hummed and picked out notes, Ella remembered a song she had played with her girlfriends in Yonkers called "Drop the Handkerchief" and the rhyme that went along with it: "A tisket, a tasket, a brown and yellow basket. I sent a letter to my mummy, and on the way I dropped it."

Later, Ella told Al Feldman, an arranger with Webb's band, about her idea of "swinging" the nursery rhyme. "They're swinging everything else—why not?" she told him. The band tried the completed version out on the Boston crowd, and the response was so good Webb decided to record it when they got back to New York. By the summer, "A-Tisket, A-Tasket" had become a smash hit; it was on the radio for weeks if you count Ella's version and others that were recorded by Fats Waller and Georgia Gibbs. At the age of eighteen, Ella had become famous both as a singer and a songwriter.

The success of the song not only made Ella Fitzgerald a household name, it also opened the way for the Webb band to play the prestigious Paramount Theater and Park Central Hotel. Their Park Central performance marked the first time that hotel had featured black performers. The largely white audiences were so enthusiastic about Ella that some of them left their seats to touch her and shake her hand. At one show, overenthusiastic fans ripped her gown.

About this time, Webb, Ella, and the vocal group The Ink Spots got their own show on NBC Radio, called "The Good Time Society." But just as it seemed Webb was beginning to achieve the kind of success that had eluded him, he became sicker and sicker. He had contracted tuberculosis of the spine and "He was always in pain, but no one ever knew it," Ella said later. While the band was playing a date at the Paramount early in 1939, Chick would sometimes faint after shows. But his determination to keep the band together and employed led him to downplay his illness. "I'm going to be so well in another couple of months," he told everyone who expressed concern.

In late spring, the band set off on a thirty-one-day tour of the South, opening with a concert on a riverboat just outside Washington, D.C. There, Webb told the band he was "taking a few days off" for a medical checkup at Johns Hopkins Hospital in his native Baltimore. Sending the band ahead on the tour, he checked into the hospital. The doctors said he had pneumonia but was too weak to treat so they sent him to his parents' home in Baltimore. There he lingered near death. After six days he told his valet to "go home and get some sleep 'cause I know I'm going." The next evening, June 16, Webb asked his mother to raise him up. Facing the group of friends and relatives who were gathered at his bedside, he grinned, jutted out his jaw, and said cockily, "I'm sorry! I gotta go!" Then the thirty-year-old bandleader died.[5]

The band was playing a concert in Montgomery, Alabama, when the news arrived. Taft Jordon recalled the scene. "I saw Ella crying. Then I saw the road manager, he was crying too. The director of the band came over to the rest of us, and he said, 'I think the man is dead.'

"We weren't thinking he meant our Chick Webb, and so we said, 'What man?' and the director said he meant Chick Webb. He was dead. We couldn't believe it.

"Anyway, after that, we cancelled bookings, and we got onto the bus and started all the way back to Baltimore, on the saddest trip I ever made."[6]

The funeral was one of the largest in the city's history. Earlier in the day, an estimated 15,000 people passed through Webb's childhood home to view his casket as Boy Scouts and members of the band stood guard. Thousands of others crowded the streets or stood on rooftops outside the church to pay their respects or catch a glimpse of the many celebrities on hand. Most stayed even when it began to rain.

During the service, the minister spoke of Webb's courage in overcoming his poverty and his handicap, of his accomplishments, and of the example he set for others. While Webb had touched many lives, his life had affected Ella's most profoundly. He had been both her adopted father and her musical mentor and she was deeply saddened by his death. But Webb's wife, Sallye, was nearly hysterical in her grief and needed Ella's help. Sitting in the front row of the church with other family members, Ella, then nineteen, held Sallye's hand and fanned her face to keep her from fainting in the intense heat.

Because music was Webb's life, the service

featured many musical selections. The band had been scheduled to play a piece, but only saxophonist Teddy McRae and pianist Tommy Fulford were composed enough to do so. They played "End of a Perfect Day" with Fulford wiping tears from his eyes in between chords.

It was only when Ella got up to sing "My Buddy" over Webb's casket that she began crying. As she half sang, half sobbed the song, she seemed so different from the smiling Ella of the bandstand that many others in the church began to cry as well. "My Buddy" was the right song for her to sing, for despite their differences—Webb outgoing and small, Ella big and shy—they shared a positive outlook on life and warm feelings for one another. As a symbol of those feelings, Webb once gave Ella a ring. "I thought it was something he wanted me to try on for size for his wife," she said, "but he said it was for me."[7]

CHAPTER FIVE

LEADER OF THE BAND

Could there be a Chick Webb band without Chick Webb? Some of the band members weren't sure. Neither was Ella, who said at the time that she "felt like quitting."

At the same time, Ella knew she needed to work now more than ever, not only to make money to support herself but also to get the love and acceptance she craved from audiences and the other members of the band.

Ella's popularity made the solution obvious to the band's management—she should become the leader. Ella became one of the youngest big band leaders in the country and also one of the few women to lead an all-male group. But since Ella really knew nothing about managing a band or choosing musical arrangements, she was the leader in name only.

"They let me conduct one number each show to make me feel I was the leader," she later recalled. But the band was actually led by other band members—at first Taft Jordon; later, Ted McRae, and then Eddie Barefield.

Ella continued to develop her singing and composing talents. In 1940, she was rewarded by being voted best female vocalist in the *Down Beat* poll for the third year in a row, leading some journalists to dub her "the first lady of song." Because of the interest in Ella's singing, the band traveled close to 20,000 miles in the year following Webb's death. Among their dates was a benefit concert that raised more than $9,000 toward a recreational center for Baltimore children that would bear Webb's name. At another concert, in New Orleans, a crowd of enthusiastic fans created a small riot in their eagerness to get Ella's autograph.

Between concerts, Ella wrote songs, picking out tunes on the piano with one finger. In 1940, she recorded two of her own compositions ("Just One of Those Nights" and "Serenade to a Sleeping Beauty") and wrote lyrics to Duke Ellington's "In a Mellotone." As a result, in 1940 she became the youngest person ever to be accepted as a member of the American Society of Composers, Authors and Publishers (ASCAP), an organization that collects royalty money for composers.

But all was not well with Ella's band. In three years, three different musicians had tried leading it but none of them could recapture the old feeling of camaraderie. Band members who had worked for low pay and endured problems on the road without complaint when Webb was in charge now were grumbling. But other problems Ella's band experienced were affecting all the bands.

By 1939, there were more big bands than ever competing for the same or even a smaller number of jobs. In 1940, some of the best music then being written was banned from the airwaves when the radio networks refused to pay songwriters the higher royalty fees ASCAP had proposed. Until ASCAP and the networks worked out an agreement almost a year later, few new songs were heard on the radio. Instead, the networks played popular songs from the 1910s and 1920s, songs whose copyrights had expired so anyone could play them for free. As a result, interest in swing sagged.

The United States' decision to enter World War II in December 1941 also had a profound impact on the music scene. Among the men who had to go off and fight were many musicians, including many from Ella's band. New regulations requiring conservation of gasoline for the war effort made touring difficult for the musicians who were left. A new entertainment tax discouraged people from going to concerts. Those who did go wanted to hear songs about their sweethearts far away, not the lively instrumental swing of their carefree, pre-war days.

To cut costs and complaints from musicians about the hardships of the road, Moe Gale teamed Ella with an instrumental combo called the Four Keys for some of her concert dates. They had one hit record ("All I Need Is You") before most of its members were drafted into the service. In the early 1940s, Ella was invited to Hollywood to sing in a movie called *Ride 'Em Cowboy* with comics Bud Abbott and Lou Costello.

Since the advent of the sound motion picture in the late 1920s, Hollywood had exploited the talents of black singers, musicians, and dancers from the New York clubs to lend sound and movement to its films. While these films helped to make performers such as Ella, Louis Armstrong, and Lena Horne better known, the roles they were given to play helped to reinforce the idea that blacks could only work in such menial jobs as servant, bellhop, janitor, and, in the case of Ella's film debut, a maid. Blacks who refused to play stereotyped roles (Horne, for instance) discovered that their scenes were cut from copies of the films shown in the South so as not to offend racist whites.

It wasn't until the nation realized its debt to blacks returning from active duty during World War II, and the National Association for the Advancement of Colored People (the NAACP—a civil rights organization) began lobbying Hollywood for better treatment, that black actors began to be allowed to play dignified and even heroic roles in films.

If *Ride 'Em Cowboy* was an inauspicious start to Ella's film career, the status of her musical career as measured by the *Down Beat* poll was downright discouraging. In 1941, Ella's orchestra was not even among the twenty-three bands cited for excellence. As a vocalist, she slipped from first to fourth place.

It was during this troubled time that Ella did something that showed just what a guiding force Webb had been—she married a shipyard worker named Benny Kornegay, someone she barely knew, just because he bet her she wouldn't do it!

"I was that stupid . . . The guys in the band were all crying when I told them," she said later.[1] The couple rented an apartment, although Ella was on the road so much she didn't spend much time there. A newspaper column at the time said Kornegay spent most of his evenings alone at home playing her records or drowning his sorrows at a bar. When Ella had the marriage annulled in 1943, even the judge scolded her. "You just keep singing 'A-Tisket, A-Tasket' and leave those men alone," he said.

The end for Ella's band—and indeed for most of the big bands—was the musicians' union strike of 1942. At that time, only singers and some bandleaders received a percentage of the profits from the use of their recordings on radio programs and in jukeboxes. American Federation of Musicians leader James Petrillo wanted all musicians to share in those royalties. To make the point clear to the record companies, he ordered all musicians to stop recording as of August 1, 1942. During the strike, which lasted for more than two years, only singers and choral groups could make records. Ella teamed up with The Ink Spots and made hit records of "Into Each Life Some Rain Must Fall" and "I'm Beginning to See the Light." After the strike, singers and choral groups such as Ella and The Ink Spots were pretty much the only musical artists well known enough to record. Between the strike and the worries of the war, people had forgotten all about the big bands. Ella's orchestra was one of the first to break up. Ella had grown up a child of the big band era and in the company of some of its most talented and caring musicians, but now a whole new musical world was opening up and Ella was going to have to face it on her own.

CHAPTER SIX

BEBOPPING

s Ella tried to figure out what to do next, she remembered something Chick Webb had told her years before: "In this business, you've always got to get there the firstest with the mostest and the newest."

Ella herself noted that "a lot of singers think all they have to do is exercise their tonsils to get ahead. They refuse to look for new ideas and new outlets, so they fall by the wayside."[1] Ella was determined not to let this happen to her.

Her first musical experiment was with a West Indian folk music known as calypso. Although the half-sung, half-spoken music was not well known in the United States, Ella went into a recording studio in 1946 and recorded a calypso song called "Stone Cold Dead in the Market" with former Webb band member Louis Jordan. The song's humorous lyrics—about a woman who hits her husband in the head with a frying pan—appealed to audiences and the song became a huge hit. One Philadelphia audience made Ella sing the song three times before they let her go on with a concert.

Even more significant was Ella's decision the next year to accept Dizzy Gillespie's invitation to go on a six-week tour. Gillespie was a trumpeter who had played with Ella's orchestra briefly in 1941 after having been fired from Cab Calloway's band (allegedly for throwing spitballs while onstage). Gillespie was known for his distinctive appearance (he had a goatee and wore thick black glasses, a beret, and bright ties) and for the exciting and sometimes controversial new jazz music he was playing called rebop, bebop, or sometimes just bop.

Developed by Gillespie, saxophonist Charlie Parker (known as Bird), pianist Thelonious Monk, and others in the early 1940s at a Harlem club called Minton's, bop was radically different from the swing music that had dominated the charts during most of the 1930s. It was much more difficult to play, containing complicated chord progressions, long strings of notes played at dazzling speed, and rhythms that were almost impossible to dance to. And it was usually played by small groups rather than big bands.

Some said bop was a musical expression of the way blacks were then feeling about the discrimination they experienced living in America. Until then, many blacks wanted nothing more than to be accepted into white society, the way Chick Webb's band had finally gotten to play at some clubs and hotels previously restricted to white entertainers. But now blacks were being more openly angry about the discrimination they had suffered. The anger burst forth in Harlem on August 1, 1943, when the rumor that a white policeman had killed a black soldier began the worst rioting in the community's history (the soldier had actually only been wounded). Now the anger was surfacing in music that, at least initially, few whites could play or understand.

This lack of understanding was reflected in the cool reception Gillespie, Ella, and the other musicians received in some of the small Southern towns they played on their 1947 tour. Recalled tour member James Moody, a saxophonist, "The people weren't quite aware of bebop and they didn't know how to dance to the music. . . . So they would stand and look up at the band as if we were nuts, you know. One time, down South, this guy was looking up and he said, 'Where's Ella Fitzgerald?' He was mad because he didn't see Ella Fitzgerald yet . . ."[2]

In fact, Gillespie may have invited Ella on the tour because of her popularity with swing and pop fans. A bop billing might not be able to draw crowds, but Ella Fitzgerald could. Ella said she agreed to go on the tour because "bop musicians have more to say than any other musicians playing today. They know what they're doing . . . I've been inspired by them and want the whole world to know it."

But how could a singer participate in a form of jazz that until then had almost always been played by instruments? Simply by singing scat. Scat is singing improvised or made-up syllables and sounds in the same way that jazz musicians improvise music on their instruments. Jazz musicians have always sung something like scat to demonstrate musical phrases to one another. But

Louis Armstrong is believed to be the first person to have sung scat as part of a recorded performance. In 1926, Armstrong was recording a song called "Heebie Jeebies" when he dropped the sheet music containing the words. Instead of trying to pick the music up and find his place, he began to sing nonsense syllables in place of the words.

Ella first tried scatting at jam sessions with the Chick Webb musicians. ". . . All the musicians would improvise on their instruments. I felt out of place until Chick suggested I improvise on my voice," she recalled. Ella can also be heard scatting a bit in her 1936 recording "Mr. Paganini." At least one jazz historian credits Ella with coining the phrase "rebop" at the close of her recording of "T'ain't What You Do, It's the Way That You Do It" in 1939.[3] Whether or not that is really the case, there's no doubt that hanging out with Gillespie and the other bop musicians on this tour took Ella's scatting skills to new heights.

"Dizzy made me want to try something with my voice that would be like a horn," Ella would later say. Gillespie encouraged Ella's efforts to sing bebop and introduced her to the song "Lady Be Good."

"When they had the all-night (radio) show, 'Make Believe Ballroom,' they used to have the musicians come on and play, and Dizzy played 'Lady Be Good' with me and we jammed. He said, 'Come on and risk this . . .' and I did . . ." Not long after, Decca recorded Ella singing the song.

A Chicago disk jockey, Dave Garroway (who later became a well-known TV host), began playing the record so often that it became a hit in

Chicago. Soon disk jockeys in other parts of the country were playing it as well. People seemed to find Ella's scat easier to enjoy than instrumental bop. Ella seemed to be having so much fun singing "Lady Be Good" that audiences couldn't help but feel the same way. The popularity of this recording and other songs she scatted on, such as "How High the Moon" and "Mack the Knife," also opened people's ears to hearing other bop music.

As a result of the tour, Gillespie and Ella were invited to headline a concert of bop at the prestigious Carnegie Hall in New York City in September 1947. After that concert, Gillespie said, "Everybody started paying attention to the music." Ella became a favorite at the New York nightclub Birdland, then known as "the jazz corner of the world," and the same jazz fans who worshiped the Bird and Diz also began seeking out Ella's records.

The tour proved to be a great personal experience for Ella, too. By this time, Ella's love of eating had become visible. Gillespie's wife, Lorraine, would cook great meals for the musicians backstage. "I remember that he [Gillespie] used to always want Lorraine to make him eggs. Everywhere we'd go, he'd want Lorraine to make him eggs," Ella said. At some theaters, "Everybody in the audience would be getting up because the food smell would be coming from backstage. They'd be getting the whiff."[4] At night, after their concert, a bunch of the musicians would go out to a nightclub and Ella and Gillespie would Lindy Hop the night away.

Among the musicians was a young bass player from Pittsburgh, Ray Brown. An early member of the bop clique that had played at Minton's, Brown played bass in the pickup band that was assembled to back up Ella for her December 1947 recording of "How High the Moon." Together with his pianist friend, Oscar Peterson, Brown developed a reputation as one of the most devoted of musicians. Recalled ex-Ellington tenor player Ben Webster, "I never saw anyone as keen on music as Oscar and Ray. They were always working on something or going over something to make it better . . . At every concert, when the curtains went down for the interval, they'd be there right behind the curtain, right through till the concert began again. They'd be at it before the concert and after it as well."

Balancing that seriousness was Brown and Peterson's love of practical jokes. According to *Jazz Anecdotes* author Bill Crow, they were forever pulling tricks on other musicians or each other, loosening a guitarist's strings or stealing the drummer's snare just before he was about to play. Once, in revenge for a trick Peterson had played on him, Brown placed a handful of little steel balls across the strings of Peterson's piano. Every note Peterson played twinged and twanged as the balls danced on the strings.

But there was apparently no joke about Brown's feelings for Ella, for shortly after the "Moon" recording session, the two began visiting each other between concert dates whenever they could.

One day, in 1948, Ella attended a concert Brown was playing in an Akron, Ohio, nightclub that changed her life. When she was recognized in the audience, fans began shouting for her to get onstage and sing. Norman Granz, the promoter in charge of the show, consented only grudgingly. He already had a singer on the show, Helen Humes, and he didn't want her to feel that she was being upstaged. But that's what happened. When Ella got up, she received some of the most enthusiastic applause of the evening and Granz decided to offer her a contract then and there. Ella accepted not long after, and that same year, she and Brown were married. It was the beginning of two of the most important relationships of Ella's life.

TOURING THE SOUTH

Depending on which date you take for Ella's birth, Norman Granz is either the same age as Ella or two years older. A native of Los Angeles, Granz had become interested in jazz while a student at the University of California at Los Angeles, and while attending concerts at nightclubs had been befriended by several musicians, including Nat King Cole and Lee Young (a brother of saxophonist Lester). Because he had heard these musicians jam together after concerts, Granz knew that some of the best music was never heard by the concert-going public. He had the idea of paying musicians to jam and inviting small audiences in to listen.

In the early 1940s, many big bands played concerts in Los Angeles, so Granz had plenty of talented people to choose from. In fact, when Ella and her orchestra were on tour in Los Angeles in 1940, Granz hired several musicians from her band—but not Ella herself! "In those days . . . I much preferred Billie Holiday," he later explained.

Granz's concerts were different not just because they revolved around jam sessions. They also were among the first to seat blacks and whites together in the audience. Granz, like Ella, had grown up in a racially mixed neighborhood, and he insisted on integration as a condition of his booking the musicians into any club. The sophisticated audiences the concerts attracted were not fazed by the mixed seating and the concerts were very successful. As Granz put it, "The club owner didn't worry about black and white once he saw the green." In 1944, Granz put on his first big concert at Philharmonic Hall in Los Angeles. He billed the event as "Jazz Concert at the Philharmonic," but when he went to put that on a poster, all the words didn't fit. So he dropped the word concert. From then on, all the concerts he put on were known by the name "Jazz at the Philharmonic."

After staging a number of successful concerts in Los Angeles, Granz decided to organize a touring group of some of the country's best jazz musicians, including Oscar Peterson and Ray Brown, and after their Akron date in 1948, Ella as well. From 1944 to 1957, they went out on the road for twenty weeks a year, visiting 100 or 120 different cities or towns in the United States and Europe.

Between tours, Ella and Ray lived in a house they had bought in the Queens section of New York City. Sometimes Ella sang with a jazz combo Brown organized and led. Eventually they began to think about having a family. Just a few years before her marriage, Ella had become national

A teenage Ella Fitzgerald singing at the Asbury Park Casino, 1938

Ella shared the spotlight with vocalist Charlie Linton when she first joined Chick Webb's band. Ella's popularity with audiences soon led Webb, here shown sitting at the drum set, to build the band's performances around Ella alone.

Connee Boswell was Ella's favorite singer while growing up. Said Ella, "Connee was actually my first singing teacher, but she never knew it."

Four great theaters from the Harlem Renaissance: (*counterclockwise*) the Harlem Opera House, the Savoy, the Apollo Theatre, and the Cotton Club

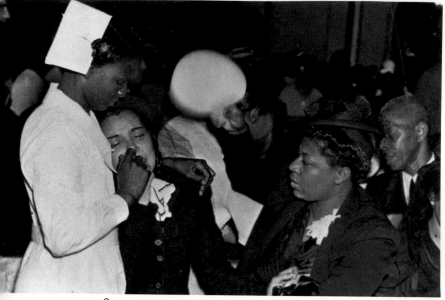

Ella Fitzgerald (*right*) at the funeral of
Chick Webb, 1939. Webb's widow,
Sallye, was overcome by grief, and is shown
here being attended by Ella and a nurse.

Over fifteen thousand mourners turned
out for Chick Webb's funeral at the
Waters African Methodist Episcopal
Church in Baltimore, Maryland.

A glamorous publicity photo of
Ella Fitzgerald in the 1930s

Ella Fitzgerald with Count Basie (*top*)
and Duke Ellington (*bottom*) at the
Savoy Ballroom in 1938

 Following Chick Webb's death, Ella became one of the youngest big band leaders in the country, and also one of the few women to lead an all-male group.

Billie Holiday, wearing her trademark gardenias

Ella Fitzgerald with the Four Keys. Ella had one big hit with this small instrumental group before most of its members were drafted during World War II.

Ella with jazz saxophonist Louis Jordan in 1947. Ella and Jordan made a hit recording of the calypso tune "Cold Stone Dead in the Market."

 Birdland, 1950. Left to right in foreground:
Oscar Pettiford, Illinois Jacquet,
Sarah Vaughan, Ray Brown, Ella

The Jazz at the Philharmonic
troupe leaves for Europe, 1956.
Left to right in foreground:
Herb Ellis, Ella, Roy Eldridge,
Gene Krupa, Flip Phillips.
Left to right, on stairs:
Illinois Jacquet, Dizzy Gillespie

Ella with Nat "King" Cole in 1957

(*Above*) Ella at the opening of the film *Pete Kelly's Blues,* in which she co-starred

(*Left*) Ella singing "Body and Soul" on "The Dinah Shore Show" in 1963

 (*Above*) Fellow artists (*left to right*) Lena Horne, Bobby McFerrin, and Quincy Jones with Ella at "Hearts for Ella," a concert to benefit the American Heart Association, 1990

 (*Facing page*) Still going strong—Ella at Avery Fisher Hall in New York City during the JVC Jazz Festival, 1987

In recent years Ella has been honored with dozens of honorary college degrees, including ones from Yale, Princeton, Dartmouth, and the Peabody Conservatory. Here she is shown receiving a doctor of music degree at Harvard's 339th commencement in 1990.

co-chairwoman of the Foster Parents Plan and began financially supporting a little boy from Naples. Having been an orphan herself, it seemed natural that Ella and her husband would decide to adopt a little boy. They named him Ray, Jr. When the Browns were on the road performing, Ella's aunt, Virginia Williams, stepped in to care for young Ray just as she had once stepped in to care for Ella.

Like the first concerts Granz organized, Jazz at the Philharmonic had a jam-session format. Musicians had considerable freedom in choosing what they played and for how long. In exchange, they were required, often against their wishes and their better musical judgment, to musically "battle" other players onstage. These portions of the concerts sometimes resembled the atmosphere of a prizefight. "Back in the early days of the tours with Norman everything was just hollering. They [the audience] didn't really listen to what you were doing; they just hollered," Ella recalled.[1]

But if musicians disliked the battling, they all appreciated the ground rules Granz set for the concerts. These included prohibitions against segregation in seating and ticket sales, and first-class accommodations for all the musicians. They appreciated it chiefly because, despite the gains blacks had made since Ella had toured with the Webb band, blacks were for the most part still treated like second-class citizens in America.

The gains included the increasing recognition won by individual black Americans in the years following World War II. Jackie Robinson became the first black to play major league baseball in 1947, Gwendolyn Brooks became the first black to win a Pulitzer prize in 1950, and Marian Anderson became the first black to sing a major role with the Metropolitan Opera in 1955. The tide of public opinion had also begun to turn more and more against discrimination, enough so that some northern and western states passed laws against it. The establishment of the federal Fair Employment Practices Commission in 1941 helped ensure fairer hiring practices, and in the mid- to late 1940s, several Supreme Court decisions attacked segregation on interstate buses and in housing practices.

But in the South, where "separate but equal" still ruled, Granz's demands were unusual, and his integrated touring troupe was not always welcome.

In fact, Granz probably missed out on thousands of dollars in bookings from concert halls and clubs that refused to have integrated seating or treat black musicians the same as whites. But, he explained, "I felt that it made no kind of sense to treat a musician with any kind of respect and dignity onstage and then make him go around to the back door when he's offstage." In fact, Granz went so far as to say one of the primary reasons he had formed Jazz at the Philharmonic was to fight discrimination. And Granz seemed to relish fighting this real-life battle almost as much as he loved staging the musical ones. Pre–civil rights movement America offered him plenty of opportunity to do both.

Ella recalled: "Once in Ohio there was a hotel that didn't want racial mixing in the rooms. Norman had everybody paired up, Oscar Peterson with Buddy Rich and so on. When the guy said that he didn't have any rooms for us, Norman went right to the NAACP and got the story on the front page of the newspaper. The hotel let that manager go because they didn't want any more bad publicity."[2]

Sometimes the Jazz at the Philharmonic musicians would mischievously switch white and black rest-room signs in bus stations, thereby creating instant desegregation. Once, in 1947, Granz and the musicians went into a restaurant that refused to serve blacks, so they stood behind the lunch counter stools in protest. About thirteen years later, black college students would adopt a similar strategy to protest segregation of eating facilities in Greensboro, North Carolina, except that instead of standing they would sit on the stools for hours. Sitting in soon became one of the most popular tactics of the civil rights movement of the early 1960s.

In the 1940s and early 1950s, however, such protests were still largely isolated acts of individual courage. But when performed by celebrities, they could have considerable impact. For example, Las Vegas was long known for its segregated theaters until former Webb band member Louis Jordan headlined a show there in 1952. Jordan was then one of the hottest performers around, and management felt they had no choice but to accede to his demand that the doors be open to blacks and whites. And the doors stayed open after he left.

Granz used different tactics to achieve the same end. In the South, where audiences were commonly segregated, he would order ticket sellers to seat blacks next to whites without the purchasers' knowledge. But when the audience was seated for one such concert in Charleston, South Carolina, people were so shocked to find themselves in a mixed audience that they kept staring at each other instead of the stage, and barely applauded for the musicians. Fearing that the musicians would be attacked by angry racists, Granz arranged for a private plane to whisk the whole troupe out of town immediately after that concert.

In July of 1954, Ella, Ella's cousin and traveling companion Georgiana Henry, and pianist John Lewis were traveling by plane from San Francisco to do some concerts in Australia when, after the plane had stopped for refueling in Honolulu, the three were told they could not continue on the flight, something that isn't supposed to happen to passengers who have first-class tickets. The group couldn't get another flight until three days later and, as a result, Ella missed several of her scheduled concerts.

The airline, Pan American, later said it had made a mistake with Ella's reservations, but early the following year Ella, Lewis, and Henry sued for racial discrimination. The matter was eventually settled out of court for $7,500.

"I think that [racial discrimination] was more of, not the airline, as much as it was someone working for the airline," Ella later said. ". . . Regardless of where you go you're going to find people like that and you can't stop a person's thinking."

Probably the most upsetting incident of this kind occurred in October of 1955 in Houston, where the Jazz at the Philharmonic troupe was playing to an integrated audience, a rare event for that city. To pass the time while waiting for their cue to go onstage, several musicians began playing dice in Ella's dressing room, while she and Henry ate and watched. But just as saxophonist Illinois Jacquet was about to roll, three white plainclothes policemen burst through the door with their guns drawn.

Hearing all the racket, Granz rushed into the room just in time to see a policeman going into Ella's bathroom. Afraid he was going to try to plant drugs there, Granz followed him and told the policeman, "I'm watching you." The policeman responded by sticking his gun into Granz's stomach and threatening to kill him. Everyone froze, and Ella and Henry began to cry. Granz said, "Well, man, you've got the gun. If you want to shoot me, there's nothing I can do about it." But instead, the cop lowered the gun and announced that they were all under arrest for gambling.[3]

Granz believed they were really arrested because Houston officials didn't like the way he had integrated the audience. "The thing was that in the South they didn't like the idea that we'd 'mix' everything. Because that sets a precedent. That's the thing they were bugged about because if you could prove that black and white could sit next to each other, you could break up a lot of (things) down there," Granz said.

Afraid that canceling the concert might provoke rioting, the police waited until a break to take Ella, Henry, Gillespie, and the others down to the station. Then the police fingerprinted them and locked them in a cell. Dizzy Gillespie was his usual cocky self. When police asked his name, he said, "Louis Armstrong." Ella was still wearing her stage outfit, a blue taffeta gown and mink stole, and crying. "I have nothing to say," she told the reporters who had somehow been alerted to the story. "What can I say? I was only having a piece of pie and a cup of coffee." She could hardly believe it when one of the policemen had the nerve to ask for her autograph!

Bail was set at $10 per person, which Granz paid in time for the troupe to return to the theater to perform the second show. A hearing was scheduled for the next day. Since they had to leave Houston to do a concert in another town, the group couldn't attend the hearing. Not showing up generally results in a police record and losing the bail money. Ella was fatalistic about it. "Let's face it, there were lots of things back then that you either had to overlook or you got angry and cried about," she later said.[4]

But Granz wasn't about to let the matter drop. The next day he called a press conference and he told the musicians' side of the story. A day later, the detective who organized the raid was demoted to a street beat. Later, Granz hired a lawyer who proved the police had no legal right to enter Ella's dressing room; the musicians got their bail money back and their police records were wiped clean. It had cost Granz $2,000 in legal fees, but the next time Granz brought an integrated concert to Houston there were no problems.

When the Jazz at the Philharmonic troupe was not fighting racial discrimination, it was making great music. As when she had toured with Webb and Gillespie, Ella learned by working with the other musicians. Granz, British jazz critic Benny Green noted, "used Ella, not as a vocal cherry stuck on top of an iced cake of jazz, but as an artist integrated thoroughly into the jam session context of the performance."

Performing with the musicians, Ella was able

to establish a reputation as a serious jazz artist in a way that singing novelty songs such as "A-Tisket, A-Tasket" failed to do. This was reflected in Ella's standing in the *Down Beat* poll, which after a decline to thirteenth in 1944 and a slow rise during the late 1940s, stood again at number one in 1953. By this time, Ella was also the acknowledged favorite of most of her musical peers. That fact was confirmed in 1960, when jazz writer Leonard Feather conducted an informal poll of 100 jazz artists to determine the greatest female jazz singers in history; Ella got 66 votes to Billie Holiday's 23. Said Bing Crosby: "Man, woman or child, Ella is the greatest. According to Frank Sinatra, "Ella Fitzgerald is as good a vocalist as anyone is going to hear for the next one hundred years."

Ella did not receive compliments well, and in fact was apt to act like a fan toward other stars. Actor Clint Eastwood recalls his meeting with Ella. "When I finally got to meet her, at a concert she was doing with Oscar Peterson, I was totally in awe of her. But to my amazement, she asked for an autographed picture of me!" Ray Brown told a similar story about an appearance she made on Bing Crosby's radio show many years earlier. "When Ella was asked to go on the show, she was so nervous she was shaking in her boots. I went to Bing's dressing room to say hello to him and to Al Jolson . . . and I found out they were nervous! I told Ella, but it made no difference; she was scared of being among people of this magnitude. She's had that ever since I met her, this lack of realization of her own importance." In fact, she once explained away the size of the crowds who came to see her in Europe by saying, "I suppose it's because they don't see us very often."

But in June 1954, an organized effort to appreciate Ella was held at the New York nightclub Basin Street. The occasion was Ella's nineteenth anniversary in the music business and among the many celebrities attending were Pearl Bailey, Eartha Kitt, Dizzy Gillespie, and Harry Belafonte. It was, *New York Times* reporter Howard Taubman said, a night when even an actress as famous as Audrey Hepburn had trouble finding a seat. Master of ceremonies Steve Allen read laudatory telegrams from those who couldn't be there. Ella also received sixteen different awards, including ones from her record company, magazines such as *Ebony* and *Jet*, the music trade newspaper *Billboard*, and many different jazz publications. While listening to the tributes, Ella displayed the delighted surprise and humility of a little girl who found more under the Christmas tree than she had ever dreamed possible. When it was time for Ella to sing, she asked to speak instead. "I guess what everyone wants more than anything else is to be loved," she said between sniffles. "And to know that you people love me and my singing is too much for me. Forgive me if I don't have all the words. Maybe I can sing it and you'll understand." Then someone put on a recording of her first smash hit, "A-Tisket, A-Tasket," and Ella went up to the mike and sang along.

But the joy of this evening was tempered by problems in Ella's personal life. Chief among these was the breakup of her marriage to Ray Brown in 1953.

On one occasion, Ella implied that her own jealousy and possessiveness might have been a factor in their breakup. "Jealousy was one of my faults before, I admit that. And I'd say jealousy comes from insecurity. I guess I haven't been really secure with any one special guy. When I was married I made mistakes: I guess all people do," she said.[5]

Despite the divorce, Ella and Brown have managed to remain friends, and even perform together on occasion. Ella said she was helped through the divorce by some advice from bandleader Duke Ellington. "I was kind of torching on the stage, crying, and he told me, 'Remember, it's like a toothache. It'll hurt you and it'll hurt you so much till finally you get rid of it. You'll miss it but you'll feel better.' "

The divorce only exacerbated a problem Ella had controlling her weight. By 1949, Ella weighed so much that when she was stranded in a stuck elevator, it took three strong men to pull her up through the trapdoor. Ella blamed the problem partly on "not being too happy as far as my love life was concerned . . . When you're happy, you're ambitious and you just want to do so much you don't have time to sit down and gorge. You're busy burning up energy. And, if you're unhappy, it's just the opposite. You sit at home and it's either TV or the ice box."[6]

The other part of the problem was simply that Ella loved to eat. Songwriter Sammy Cahn remembers seeing Ella at a recording session in 1938. "She was standing at the microphone with a hot dog in one hand, and a bottle of Coke in the other. It was a ballad she was about to record, a song that required some kind of feeling, some personal involvement. She couldn't wait to [finish] the song so she could eat."[7] In later years, she would start collecting cookbooks from all over the world. Reading them, she says, is "like reading love stories—you find yourself comparing what different cooks will do with the same meats. Doreen, my housekeeper, makes fish like nobody else—she rolls it and cooks it in dill, with a special sauce."

Whatever the causes, the effect of her excess poundage was to make her more inhibited onstage. As a former aspiring dancer, Ella loves to move while she sings. "There are things I would like to do when I'm onstage, but I'm afraid that if I do them they wouldn't make sense because people would ask: 'What's she doing that for?' She's not supposed to do that . . . I'm insecure because I feel I'm not glamorous enough," she said.

In the early 1950s, Ella also began to feel increasingly dissatisfied with her recording company and management. In 1935, Ella had signed with Decca, one of three major recording companies operating at the time and one known to be chiefly interested in getting rich quick on hit records. In her nearly twenty years with the company, Ella's records had sold 22 million copies in spite of, rather than because of, the songs she was given to sing. Music critics were nearly unanimous in their belief that Decca executive favorites like "Melinda the Mousie," "My Wubba Dolly," "Santa Claus Got Stuck in My Chimney," and "The Bean Bag Song" did not show off Ella's talent to its best advantage.

As early as her Chick Webb days, Ella had loved ballads, but Decca didn't often give her the chance to sing them. "There are so many pretty songs I could sing on records . . . Yet, I never do

get a chance at the songs that have a chance . . .
I don't know what they're doing at that record
company," she said.

Tim Gale, a booking agent who worked with
Ella for many years, tells another story, one about
a star who had trouble sticking by her own decisions. After complaining about the songs she was
given, she would sing them anyway if her advisers insisted. And Gale said her advisers were often right.

"One of her records was a thing called 'Hap-
piness.' She cut it under protest. I brought the dub
backstage to her at the Paramount, and she said,
'It's a shame. A corny performance of a corny
song.' " But, Gale said, the song turned out to be
a big hit.

Gale recalled another time when Ella was doing a concert and an audience member began
hounding her to sing "Mule Train," then a big hit
for Frankie Lane. Finally Ella gave in, but because
she was angry, she sang it in such a way that she
was sure he'd never ask for it again. According to
Gale, Ella "proceeded to do a burlesque so tre-
mendous that she kept it in the act and scored
riotously with it everywhere."[8]

The music Ella performed with Jazz at the Philharmonic might have been of a higher quality,
but it was heard only by those who attended the
concerts. Granz was one of the first jazz produc-
ers to capture the sounds of jazz concerts on live
recordings on his own label, Verve, but because
Ella was still under contract to Decca, he had to
cut out all of Ella's contributions.

Talent scout John Hammond had once tried
to get Ella to switch to a different recording company, but her manager, Moe Gale, asked for

more money than Hammond was able to afford. Hammond said he later heard Gale had re-signed Ella to Decca for a much lower fee. Whether or not this was true, it was not uncommon for managers to cheat their stars in those days, either by actively stealing or by simply keeping them in the dark about much of their business dealings. This was especially true when the stars were black and the managers were white.

The most frequently cited example of a white manager exploiting the talents of a black musician involves Irving Mills and his client Duke Ellington. In addition to forming a company giving himself the same share of profits from Ellington's music that Ellington himself received, Mills put his name on many of Ellington's songs for merely making a few suggestions and editing changes. By the late 1930s, other blacks began to publicly chide Ellington for putting up with such an unfair arrangement.

"No negro writer has written the lyrics for any of Duke Ellington's melodies since he has been under the Mills banner. What's the matter, Duke? House rules?" one writer challenged in the black newspaper *The Pittsburgh Courier.*

But racism and the fact that the recording, the-atrical, and broadcast industries were run almost entirely by whites meant that black entertainers often had no choice but to seek white help. While there is no doubt that Irving Mills became rich from Duke Ellington's music, Ellington did, too. By contrast, Jelly Roll Morton, King Oliver, and many other black performers who refused white management died poor and forgotten.

Ella had been with Moe Gale since her Chick

Webb days, but in the 1940s, Gale's agency merged with Joe Glaser's, and Glaser took her on. Joe Glaser was a white man who had a large clientele of famous black artists, including Louis Armstrong, Billie Holiday, Pearl Bailey, and Sarah Vaughan. According to Armstrong biographer James Lincoln Collier, Glaser treated his clients as children and didn't trust them with much of their own money. Glaser reportedly safeguarded about half of Armstrong's earnings. Glaser would buy musicians' contracts from other managers without the musicians' knowledge or consent. Jazz trumpeter Roy Eldridge once had to make weekly deductions from his salary with Gene Krupa's band to get out of such an indentured servitude to Glaser. But Ella at least knew the score. When a teenage Sarah Vaughan made her debut at the Apollo Theatre on a bill Ella was headlining in 1943, Ella took her aside backstage to tell her to beware of dishonest managers and agents.

Throughout the weeks and months of touring with Jazz at the Philharmonic, Granz had more than proven himself trustworthy. In fact, Ella probably had not respected anyone as much since Chick Webb had died, which is not to say that Granz and Ella agreed on everything. Granz concedes that Ella thought he was "too much of a blowtop." Indeed, during the course of their long business relationship, the two have had some whopping fights. But when Granz asked Ella if he could take on the management of her career in 1954, the terms he offered were those of friends: There would be no contract, just a handshake, and he would work the first year for free. She agreed to all the terms except for his not being paid.

Granz's first job as Ella's manager was to try and get her out of her contract with Decca. At first, Granz did no better than Hammond. Then, one day in 1955, Granz learned that Decca was planning to release the soundtrack to a film biography of Benny Goodman. The film featured Gene Krupa and Stan Getz, two musicians under exclusive contract to Granz. Granz waited until the record was just about to be released before telling Decca it needed his permission to release the record—and the only way to get it was to let Ella out of her contract. Backed into a corner, Decca agreed. Now Granz would have charge over what Ella recorded as well as where and when she sang. His ideas about her recordings would have a profound impact on her career.

THE SONGBOOKS

One of Granz's first recommendations to Ella after becoming her manager was that she should expand her repertoire. While Granz respected Ella's jazz abilities, he felt that there would be a much bigger audience for her talents if she sang more popular songs. Not the Tin Pan Alley trash Decca had forced on her, but quality songs worthy of her talents.

In 1953, just five years after the long-playing record was invented, Frank Sinatra had recorded a collection of songs from Broadway musicals which had given a jumpstart to his career. Granz thought these types of songs might also work well for Ella. He proposed a series of songbook albums, each one devoted to the works of a different Broadway composer.

Ella was skeptical. "At first I thought, 'What is he trying to do, ruin me?' " she said. For seven years she had devoted her career to singing bebop. "I thought that bop was it. That all I had to do was go some place and sing bop." But by the 1950s, the jazz scene had begun to shift from bop to a new school of jazz known as California cool, and Ella noted, "It finally got to the point where I had no place to sing. I realized then that there was more to music than bop."

So, despite her reservations, Ella decided to go along with the first project Granz proposed: a collection of songs by Cole Porter. A witty and sophisticated composer who had attended Yale, Porter worked in the Broadway theater of the twenties and thirties writing such now well-known songs as "Night and Day" and "I've Got You Under My Skin." As good as Porter's songs were, they were often forgotten as soon as the show he had written them for flopped or closed.

Ella was not very familiar with Porter's work. Granz picked all the songs, and Ella admitted later, "I hardly knew what I was going to be sing-ing till I got to the studio . . . Sometimes it's fun to record like that, but often you wish that you knew the songs a little bit better. When you hear the final recording, you think, 'If I had really known the song, I would have tried this, or I would have done that.' "

When the albums came out, a few critics did complain that Ella didn't sound as if she knew or understood the words. It was a criticism Ella had heard as far back as "A-Tisket, A-Tasket." (Some said that song came across as awfully cheerful for a song that was about someone losing some-thing they loved.) Composer Dave Frishberg an-swered that charge this way: "A lot of people say that Ella Fitzgerald doesn't sing with meaning, that she doesn't understand what she's singing.

Yet when I listen to her sing that songbook series—these are the definitive versions. Maybe it's because she doesn't attempt to imbue each line with special meanings and everything, she's just treating it as a musical phrase to be sung in a musical and economical way, [so] the song comes right across."

Singing the Cole Porter material demanded that Ella stifle a great deal of her natural instinct for jazz improvisation and rhythms. This sophisticated music demanded a simpler treatment. As Ella explained, "I've tried not to put too much jazz in some of the songs because the lyrics don't call for it."

Jazz critic Nat Hentoff said he believed Ella's long-standing reticence to reveal aspects of her personal life made her even more ideally suited to sing popular music than the more emotionally demanding jazz. Moreover, Hentoff wrote, "Unlike other singers who have deliberately 'condescended' to sing 'hit' material, Ella likes most pop ballads—if they're gentle and innocent enough. It's partly because she is so honestly a resident of the pop world that she can sing most pop songs so much better than her contemporaries. . . . She not only has the necessary belief in the material to project to her audience, but she also has such superior musicianship."

Before the Cole Porter album was released, Granz took the edited tapes of the album to Porter, then an invalid living at the Waldorf Towers in New York. Porter was known to be very critical of performances of his work. He listened in silence as Granz played all thirty-two tracks of the album. Then he turned to Granz and said simply, "What diction she has." Many years later, Ella would receive the Cole Porter Centennial "You're the Top" Award for "outstanding achievements for sustaining the Cole Porter legend and for winning new audiences to an appreciation of a genius." When she released an album of the Broadway tunes of George and Ira Gershwin a few years later, Ira said, "I never knew how good our songs were until I heard Ella Fitzgerald sing them." Chimed in Richard Rodgers, another composer of an Ella songbook: "Whatever it is Ella does to my songs, they sound better."

Broadway composers had good reason to like Ella's songbook albums. They were the first to give composers billing equal to the artist, and they created interest in songs that had been forgotten. The composers were not only now collecting royalty money because of Ella, but also because of the other artists who heard her singing them and wanted to record them as well.

But Ella worried that she was alienating her old jazz fans with this new direction. When she first began to sing the new songs in concerts, she would search for Granz sitting in the hall, hoping to get some encouragement from the expression on his face. One night Granz and Ella had a big fight after a concert at which she was supposed to sing "April in Paris." Instead she let the audience shout her into changing to one of her old bop tunes, "Lady Be Good."

"When she came offstage she yelled at me and I yelled louder at her, and we didn't speak to one another for three days," Granz said.[1] The incident was reminiscent of other fights Ella and Granz had when, responding to audience applause, Ella would sing many more songs than were on the program she and Granz had agreed to. "Sometimes we'd argue and wouldn't speak for weeks on end, and he'd give me messages through a third party," Ella recalled.

But sales of 100,000 copies of *The Cole Porter Songbook* convinced her the songbooks were the way to go. When jazz fans asked, "What's the matter, Ella, you goin' square?," she defended her choice. "I'm not going square, I'm going versatile," she explained. Later she recalled how "some people thought maybe I shouldn't do them, or couldn't do them, so it was a challenge . . . I was learning something new and becoming someone else." Within a month, *The Cole Porter Songbook* became the eleventh best-selling album in America in 1956. Ella called it "the turning point of my life."

During the next twelve years Ella paid musical tribute to Rodgers and Hart, Irving Berlin, Jerome Kern, Harold Arlen, Johnny Mercer, and the Gershwins among other composers. Because many of the people who bought the songbooks had never heard these composers' music or jazz before, they brought new audiences to the music. The songbooks also increased audiences for Ella. Jazz clubs had been half-full when she played before the albums were released now had to turn people away. "Now in addition to jazz singing, I had something to offer people who wanted to hear the pretty songs," she explained.

Places that had never featured jazz singers began to book her as well. Ella was invited to perform at the Mocambo, a swanky Hollywood supper club, at the urging of actress Marilyn Monroe, who had heard her perform for two nights at a smaller place. Following the standing-room-only success of that engagement, Ella became the first jazz performer to entertain in the Venetian Room of San Francisco's Fairmont Hotel. To gain that booking, Granz told the hotel he would make up for any loss of income caused by Ella's engagement. Instead, both Ella and the hotel ended up making money. While on the West Coast, she appeared in her second movie, *Pete Kelly's Blues,* a story of jazz musicians who become involved with gangsters, directed by "Dragnet" TV series star Jack Webb. He cast Ella in a featured role and gave her two songs, including the title song. Today the film has achieved cult status for its excellent score. She was also featured at big Las Vegas nightclubs such as the Flamingo, and at the first major American jazz festival, held in Newport, Rhode Island.

In New York City, she played the Waldorf-Astoria and became the first black artist to headline a bill at the Copacabana nightclub. The last line of the *Variety* review of the latter concert read, "Add the Copa to Miss Fitzgerald's kayo [knockout] list."

Television was just coming into its own at about this time, and Ella made appearances on variety shows headlined by Garry Moore, Nat King Cole, Ed Sullivan, and Frank Sinatra. She made her symphony orchestra debut when Arthur Fiedler, a fan of her recording of "Too Darn Hot," hired her to sing it with the Boston Pops, and followed it up in 1958 with an appearance at the Hollywood Bowl with a symphony orchestra before an audience of some 22,000 people.

Ella was once again popular enough to headline tours of her own. Granz was so busy managing her career that, in 1957, he decided to discontinue all other work but the international tours of Jazz at the Philharmonic.

Prompted by her success with the songbooks, Ella recorded multiple-disk albums with jazz colleagues Duke Ellington and Louis Armstrong. Although Ella loved working with both Ellington and Armstrong, her collaborations with these great artists did not result in her most successful songbooks. Ella had been charmed by the Duke's suave manner and sophisticated music since they appeared together at the Apollo Theatre in 1943. But recording the Ellington album proved to be a hectic business.

Because he didn't have time to write new arrangements of his songs for the album, Ellington used his regular big band scores and instructed Ella to sing her solos where the instrumental choruses normally went. As a result, the instrumentalists got all the good solos. The Ellington songbook does contain evidence of the Duke's fondness for Ella in the form of a sixteen-minute song in four movements called "A Portrait of Ella Fitzgerald." And the release of this album was launched by a prestigious joint concert at Carnegie Hall in 1958.

During the latter part of the 1950s, Ella recorded three albums with Louis Armstrong: *Ella and Louis, Ella and Louis Again,* and *Porgy and Bess.* By then Armstrong was beginning to be treated as the legendary jazz figure he was. Ella had long admired Armstrong for both his trumpet playing and landmark gravelly-voiced singing. In fact, in about 1950 Ella had recorded a version of "Basin Street Blues" with a chorus in which she imitated Louis's singing—in the same way Taft Jordan had done in Chick Webb's Band. The tribute was so convincing that some of her fans thought that recording was the first album she and Louis made together.

Unfortunately, Armstrong was tired and overworked when they recorded *Ella and Louis.* His lip was so weak from overuse that he had to sing many songs he had originally been planning to play; when he did play, it was out of only one side of his mouth. To help Armstrong, Ella sang all the songs in his keys rather than ones that would have been more suited to her voice.

The only other sour note sounding at the time was an emergency operation Ella had to undergo in 1957 for an abdominal abscess. While in the middle of a performance at the Paramount Theater in New York, she fell ill and had to be rushed to the hospital. An even more unusual incident happened while Ella was doing a concert at the Warner Theater in Atlantic City, New Jersey. Ella was in the middle of a song when a former mental patient suddenly leapt on stage and punched her in the jaw. The man's last name was Fitzgerald, although he was no relation of Ella's. Fortunately, Ella was not hurt seriously.

An incident in London angered her much more. While on an international tour with the Jazz at the Philharmonic troupe in 1958, Ella and the entire group of musicians were detained in a London airport for hours while customs officials thoroughly searched their baggage and clothes. They slit Granz's toothpaste tube, checked inside instruments, examined the lining of Ella's coat, and even had a bottle of Ray Brown's vitamins sent to a lab for analysis. After going through all six of Ella's suitcases and not finding anything, one customs man asked Ella if she had anything else "on her person." Ella replied, "Yeh, buster. I'm a big girl not likely to be mistaken for Marilyn Monroe and I wear a girdle."[2]

Despite this, the years between 1955 and 1960 were generally good ones for Ella because it was a time when she felt increasingly loved and accepted. "It just seemed that more people began to like my singing. The awards I began winning . . . made me realize people loved me," she said later. In fact, in 1958, Ella won the top honor in the recording industry, the Grammy Award, for *The Irving Berlin Songbook.* It was the first year the award was given, making Ella the first black woman ever to receive a Grammy. The Grammy is a trophy replica of an old-time phonograph called a gramophone that is awarded by a vote of composers, musicians, and music industry executives from across the country.

Ella's *Duke Ellington Songbook* also won a Grammy and many of the other songbooks are considered definitive versions of their composers' works. But many critics believe the best of the songbooks was the one devoted to the songs of George and Ira Gershwin. The recording session for those albums was preceded by a year of discussions among Granz, album musical director Nelson Riddle, and Ira Gershwin.

In addition to the regular fifty-three song, five-album sets, *The Gershwin Songbook* was also released in a limited edition of 175 copies, each signed by Ella, Ira Gershwin, Nelson Riddle, and Bernard Buffet, the artist who created original lithographs for the record sleeves. They were sold for $100 then, and if you could find one today, probably would cost ten times that. In his spare time, Granz was a collector of modern art and the limited edition was his way of saying that Ella's work was on a par with that of the greatest of visual artists. The public apparently agreed, for in a month, these albums were sold out.

CHAPTER NINE

DISCORD

Thanks to the songbooks and the demand they created for personal appearances, Ella tripled her income between 1955 and 1959. As great as it was to be popular again, it also meant that in the late fifties and early sixties, Ella worked harder than she ever had. For as many as forty-eight weeks a year she traveled around the globe. Tours often took her to different cities, hundreds of miles apart, on successive evenings.

"On the Continent [of Europe] we were sometimes at the second concert until 3 A.M.—in Frankfurt it was 4:30—and then had to get up early to catch a plane," she recalled. "In Amsterdam we did a midnight show, then flew to Warsaw to appear that night." The most time she ever had free was two weeks, although, more often than not, she said, "It was off to Australia or Europe or

Japan or South America. Instead of having vacations, we'd wind up going to another country [to sing]."

Traveling with Gillespie and the Jazz at the Philharmonic troupe Ella had been able to relax by playing cards with band members (she is a whiz at rummy and blackjack), taking naps, or going to the movies. But traveling on her own at this new pace was not as much fun. Sometimes she got lonely; she especially missed spending time with her son.

"I'd sure like to be [home] fiddlin' around in the kitchen making Ray things to eat," she said in a 1957 interview. She was often tired, and she worried that as a result, her performances were suffering.

"Let's face it, when you're traveling all the time and don't get enough rest, sometimes the voice is tired and you look tired and you don't feel that you're up to doing a show, and yet you've got to go out there. You've always got to run the risk of having someone say: 'She's supposed to be the greatest, but she gets away with anything. She's not singing.' . . . When you've done so well so long and won so many honors, it gives you the feeling that the first time you do one little thing wrong, people are going to be down on you," she said.[1]

Guitarist Barney Kessel once tried to analyze why Ella felt this way. "I think she lays so much stress on being accepted in music because this is the one area of life into which she feels she can fit successfully. Her marriages failed; she doesn't have an awful lot of the normal activities most women have, such as home life, so she wraps herself up entirely in music. She wants desperately to be accepted."

Whatever the reason, Ella's feelings of uncertainty about her own performances sometimes made it difficult for her to share the spotlight with others.

In his book *Jazz People,* writer Dan Morgenstern said that when Roy Eldridge was featured in Ella's accompanying group "she seldom gave him solos to play, and if he got a big hand, she would cut out the offending solo spot forthwith." Morgenstern also noted that "A negative comment in a review, no matter how unimportant the publication or how slight the criticism, is capable of reducing her to tears . . ."

When Frank Sinatra criticized her phrasing and breathing in a *Life* magazine article in 1965, Ella became so upset, she said, "I could hardly sing for a week. . . . I was beginning to be afraid, I felt maybe I just didn't have it."

Ella always had a problem with nervousness before going onstage. "I go through that same old grief every time—my legs turn to water and a million butterflies play tag in my stomach," she said. "The only thing is, if you're a professional you just don't let it show." But in 1957 at the Newport Jazz Festival, it did show. Normally quick to take the blame for mistakes during concerts, she became noticeably upset with a drummer who was having trouble staying on the beat, and with a sound man when her microphone began squealing. Even during a concert when things went relatively smoothly, her lack of ease onstage was noticeable to critics such as John S. Wilson of the *New York Times,* who called her between-song chatter "rote" and said she seemed to use songs "to protect herself from the audience."

Press people such as Wilson were one of Ella's pet peeves. Shy and reserved with anyone she doesn't know, Ella dislikes doing interviews. Her press agent at the time, Virginia Wicks, explained, "She can come over to the house and we'll exchange small talk and she's just as sweet and charming as can be. Then I'll gingerly try to ease the conversation around to, say, a *Life* or *Time* man who wants to see her and her face will fall and she'll stomp her foot and (with an expression not unlike the little girl in "A-Tisket, A-Tasket" when she says, No, no, no!) say, 'Gosh darn it, Virginia, I can't do it—I have to go shopping!' "

Reporters she did talk to sometimes found her difficult. An interview Maurice Burman tried to conduct with her for the English magazine *Melody Maker* in 1958 is illustrative. Meaning to pay her a compliment, he opened the interview by asking, "What does it feel like to be perfection?"

"I am not perfection. I am far from perfect, but I always try to improve," she replied.

"As a matter of fact, I have heard you breathe in the middle of a word . . . ," Burman teased. "The word is 'gliding' and the record is 'Manhattan.' "

"What!" Ella said in dismay. "I've never noticed it—no one's ever told me that before."

Turning to some photographers who had been taking pictures and shouting for her to turn this way and that, she said, "I can only do one thing at a time. I can't look in all directions at once. And you," she added, turning to Burman, "let me finish one question before you ask me the next."

Reporters who didn't know anything about her career or asked her the same old questions—such as to list her favorite singers—put her off. So did questions about her personal life, which she considered prying.

She was more comfortable with fans. In 1987, Ella was spotted sitting in a store one day looking "my worst; I had my sneakers on and an old skirt" when a woman recognized her and "stopped and said, 'We love you,' and then another girl came and soon everybody was asking me for autographs. I said to myself 'Well, you can't beat this kind of love . . .' "

But even interruptions like these were not always welcome. Once in New York City, when a man approached her for an autograph on the street, where she had stopped to get a hot dog for lunch, Ella very politely told him he was mistaken: She was not Ella Fitzgerald. Then she went back to eating her hot dog.

Said Jimmy Rowles, a former accompanist, "People bother her. So she leaps into limos and disappears. She has things on her mind to do. And as a legend, her life doesn't belong to her. So it's hard for her to escape when she's going through a hotel lobby filled with autograph seekers."[2]

When Granz became her manager, he assumed much of the burden of dealing with the public. "The idea was, get him to do the talking for me and I'd do the singing. I needed that," she said. But in the early 1960s, just as her increased popularity made the pressures on her most intense, Granz decided to sell his record company, Verve, to MGM Records (for a reported $2.75 million) and move to Geneva, Switzerland.

CHAPTER TEN

INTER-
MISSION

Granz has never spoken publicly about why he moved, but several things going on in the country at the time could have affected his decision. One was the increasing commercial success of rock and roll, demonstrated most dramatically by Elvis Presley when he returned from the U.S. Army to record two hit records, "It's Now or Never" and "Are You Lonesome Tonight." The other was a congressional investigative committee's disclosure of corruption in the record industry. Disk jockeys were playing certain records in exchange for illegal bribes from record company executives. Granz was not involved, but the scandal probably angered him.

Granz also was disappointed by the time it was taking the U.S. government to make progress on behalf of civil rights. In 1954, in the landmark case *Brown vs. the Board of Education of Topeka*, the Supreme Court ruled that compulsory education in public schools denied equal protection under the law. This decision effectively overturned the "separate but equal" argument that had been used to justify segregation since 1896.

Although it applied only to education, *Brown vs. the Board of Education* inspired blacks to seek an end to all sorts of discriminatory practices. One Montgomery, Alabama, woman's refusal to give up her bus seat to a white man in 1955, and her resulting arrest, prompted a year-long boycott of buses by city blacks. In 1960, college students began sit-in protests in restaurants, and in 1963, the Reverend Martin Luther King, Jr., led nonviolent protest marches in Birmingham, Alabama, and Washington, D.C. All along the way, these peaceful protesters were met with violent resistance from local government officials and racist whites, especially in the South. Some activists were killed or beaten or had their houses burned to the ground. When racists bombed a Birmingham church, four young girls were killed.

Congress responded to the crisis by passing the Civil Rights Act of 1964, a bill that outlawed discrimination in public places and in employment. But for many blacks in the North, it was too late. Impatient with the slow progress of legal remedies, and overwhelmed by economic and social problems that legislation did not address, blacks in Harlem, Los Angeles, Detroit, and Newark, New Jersey, struck back by burning and looting their own inner-city neighborhoods in riots that took place in 1964, 1965, and 1967.

Ella was certainly aware of all the civil rights

activities. It was impossible to live in America then and not be aware. But as one of the few blacks to have achieved success in white America, she was not as in touch with the issues as less privileged blacks. The civil rights movement also increased in intensity during one of the busiest times in her career. Although Ella is patriotic and speaks with pride of her meetings with presidents Johnson and Reagan, she had never been interested in politics. She did speak admiringly of Martin Luther King, Jr., however, and donated concert proceeds to a foundation dedicated to his memory after his 1968 assassination. "He made it so instead of fighting, people now talk, and it's so much easier," she said.

Of more immediate concern to Ella was the effect the rising popularity of rock and roll and soul might have on her career. Ella was kept well informed about the contemporary music scene by Ray Jr., sixteen, who played drums in a Beatles-like combo on weekends, and a fourteen-year-old niece. During interviews at the time, she expressed admiration for the Beatles and the Monkees, and later for Carole King, Randy Newman, Paul Williams, and Stevie Wonder. She even wrote a musical tribute to drummer Ringo Starr, which read, in part, "Don't knock the rhythm of the kids today; remember they're playing the Ringo way." Whenever a new pop song was written that she thought she could perform, she would introduce it into her act.

"I try to change. I don't like to be at a standstill," she once explained. "I love jazz because it's part of me, but I also want to do some other things." Why? Once again, it was Ella trying to "satisfy everybody," as she puts it. Everybody, that is, but some critics who said that the "Love Boat" theme song, "Ode to Billie Joe," and some of the other modern songs she tackled were not ideally suited to her talents.

Whether Ella championed the new sounds or not, there was no doubt that the American public liked them. Not only were the new rock artists playing in large stadiums instead of concert halls, they also dominated the record business, including Granz's old label, Verve. Almost immediately after buying Verve, the new owners set out to eliminate many of Granz's jazz artists and records in order to make room for new rock groups such as the Velvet Underground and the Mothers of Invention. During the sixties, only Ella and a handful of Granz's other jazz stars continued to record for Verve. But without any hit records, Ella said, "I just began to feel like, well, I don't have it, you know. . . . There's nothing worse in life for a performer than to go out there and do nothing with an audience. I'm very self-conscious about people not liking me."[1]

In the spring of 1965, in the middle of a European tour of one-nighters, the pressures and insecurities mounted to the point where Ella felt she couldn't take it anymore. Onstage in Munich, Ella stopped singing and had to be led offstage in a daze. Backstage she almost literally began to climb the walls. She was able to regain her composure in time to finish the concert, but her doctor warned that she had been near an emotional breakdown and badly needed to take some time off. "You can get in a bad situation," she said as she reflected on the experience later that year. "The audiences are wonderful and you don't want to turn down the jobs, so you suddenly come to realize that you're working too hard to enjoy yourself . . . Sometimes you find you're way up on top and all by yourself. It can get lonely up there and you miss all the kicks . . . Instead of enjoying the singing and the entertaining, you find it becomes just a thing of how much can I get out of it."[2]

Ella had purchased a house in Beverly Hills, California, in 1957. She went there following the incident in Munich, and stayed there for most of 1965. Her favorite relaxations during those months included cooking, going to the movies, shopping for the house, sewing, watching television (especially baseball games), listening to records, and taking music and language lessons. As a teenager in the Webb band, she had tried playing the accordion. Now she was interested in learning how to play vibes and guitar. She studied Spanish and French, but just as she had done when a little girl taking piano lessons, she was distracted by how her teacher looked. "My teacher was . . . so handsome I didn't learn a thing. He'd walk in with the simpatico look. Then we'd have sandwiches and Napoleon brandy, and before I knew it the lesson was over."

Ella also enjoyed visiting with relatives and a few close friends. By this time, a substantial number of Ella's aunts, cousins, and nieces and nephews had relocated to the Los Angeles area. In fact, after the death of Ella's sister (actually a half sister whom she had not grown up with), Ella took in several of her half sister's five children. While she was on tour, Ella's aunt, Virginia Williams, cared for them as well as Ray, Jr.

At the time, Ella talked about wanting to get

back to performing in less intimidating small clubs, and getting a television show so she could live at home more. But neither of these things happened. Ella also talked about wanting to remarry, and although rumors circulated in the late forties and fifties that she had been secretly wed to a Norwegian, they were only rumors. For four years in the mid-sixties she did rent an apartment just outside Copenhagen, "because I had a romance there," she said. Today the Danish furniture in her home is a reminder of that relationship.

Meanwhile, from his home in Europe, Granz followed the way MGM was treating the artists he had signed for Verve and became more and more angry.

"It's criminal that someone like Sarah Vaughan was allowed to go without making a single record for five years. It's an outrage that of the twenty-seven albums I produced with Art Tatum for Verve, not a single one is available—they've all been deleted from the catalog. . . ." Granz said.[3]

Eventually Granz became so disgusted that he offered to buy back Verve. MGM refused. So, in 1972, Granz started another record label, naming it Pablo in honor of Pablo Picasso, one of his favorite painters. Like his early pioneering offerings at Verve, many of the Pablo releases featured jazz artists in live performance at concerts or jazz festivals. On Pablo records, Ella frequently teamed up with Oscar Peterson, Count Basie, and Joe Pass (she won her eighth and tenth Grammy Awards for records with Basie and Pass) and even tried her hand at the Latin sounds of Antonio Carlos Jobim.

To support the release of these albums, Ella resumed touring on a more regular schedule. But during this time, she was diagnosed as having a cataract, a slight film over the eye that obstructs vision. It was removed during an operation that was considered to be completely successful. "I can reach [audiences] now and see how happy they feel," she said shortly after the cataract was removed. But a year later, while Ella was performing in Nice, her right eye hemorrhaged, a complication of the operation brought on by several health problems, including diabetes, that Ella had not known she had. Once again, Ella was sidelined as she underwent laser treatments that probably saved her sight. With the help of thick tinted glasses, she was able to have 20/20 vision in one eye.

When Ella returned to work eight months later, she worried about her fans' reaction to her tinted glasses. "I was afraid people would laugh at me . . . But nobody paid the slightest bit of attention, so it was O.K."

However, her eye problems have made her extra sensitive to smoke and bright lights such as news photographers' flashbulbs. "If they shoot close to where I had that hemorrhage, the moment that flashbulb hits, it's as if someone punched me in the eye," she has said. Once, when she was doing a benefit for a musicians' union in Pennsylvania, a photographer continued to take pictures of her even though she asked him not to. Finally, the pain was so bad she began hitting him and trying to take the camera away. "I felt so bad about it afterward because people like that don't mean any harm," she said later.[4]

There was sorrow for Ella that year. On July 6, 1971, Louis Armstrong died. Ella had been named one of the honorary pall bearers. But she only sat quietly through the service, and left quickly when it was over. "Everyone came looking to perform," said jazz producer George Wein. "[But Ella] wasn't looking for publicity. She's that kind of person."

Three years later, Duke Ellington was gone as well. Ella was stunned. "You knew his death had to come sometime, I guess, but I'd known him ever since I was a girl," she said. People cried when Ella sang at Chick Webb's funeral; they did again at the Duke's when she sang "In My Solitude" and "A Closer Walk with Thee."

"I have the feeling I was singing the wrong words but all I knew was that where I was standing I could look right across at his body and I was sort of frozen," she said later.

By this time the jazz world had also lost such greats as Billie Holiday and Charlie Parker, both to alcohol and drugs. Ella, in contrast, didn't smoke, had never used drugs, and drank nothing more than an occasional glass of wine. Record producer Rosetta Reitz believes this is because Ella had always been taken care of. "Chick Webb was very protective of Ella . . . And Norman Granz later on was very protective. Maybe, like so many singers, her love-life was kind of disappointing, but her work hasn't been ruined . . ." she said.[5]

Nevertheless, the deaths of her friends and her own health problems gave Ella pause. "When something like this happens, it makes you stop and say to yourself: 'Where am I going? What am I doing—for myself and for others?' It kind of makes you think," she said. "So I say to myself, 'Well, I'm only seeing out of one eye now, but God gave me a voice. He gave me something with which to make other people happy. There must have been a reason.' "

CHAPTER ELEVEN

ON STAGE

At the peak of her career, Ella spent forty-eight weeks of the year in concerts around the world. Most of her public life and some of her happiest moments have taken place on stage. Her performances also provide the best way to understand her artistry.

A typical concert is preceded by a rehearsal late in the afternoon to check the sound system. Ella steps up to the microphone exactly at the scheduled time and hits the first note. As she sings, technicians adjust the microphone levels.

"I sound thin. Do I sound thin?" she might ask anxiously after reaching for her first high note of the day. After flubbing the words to a song, she might apologize, "Sorry, fellas, that was my fault." Her band members rarely make mistakes. Ella knows enough to pick the very best musicians, and they stay with her so long they develop a sixth sense about what she wants. Waiting for her pianist, the conductor, and some musicians to finish conferring about a song, Ella might begin singing in an Elmer Fudd voice, just for fun. A musician quickly jumps in with an appropriate accompaniment and everyone laughs. But soon it's back to business. Nobody talks much. There's no need to. They're saying all they need to with the music.

How does Ella choose her songs? How does she figure out how to sing them? Ella has never seemed to like to answer this question. "I just sing as I feel, man. Jazz ain't intellectual," she told one newspaper reporter. But Ella's long-time piano accompanist and arranger, Tommy Flanagan, once explained how she works in more detail.

"Sometimes Ella comes up with a tune that she's heard somewhere, or I may send her a song that I feel is especially right for her. Then we get together to find a key she's comfortable in. She tells me how she feels this piece should be done— serious or playful and humorous—the kind of mood it communicates to her. I then work up an orchestration that embodies her ideas and my own and we try it together."

But, Flanagan warns, with any singer as creative as Ella, the arrangements are "only a framework within which to move. She will still do all kinds of things within that framework. Often she'll add a new twist or improvisation, even when we're actually on stage performing. She may lag behind the beat a bit or move ahead of it, but she always knows exactly what she is doing. What would be musically risky for some singers, she pulls off easily. She rarely sings a song exactly the same way she did it last. But we've all played together for so long that no matter what she does, we are all right there together."[1]

Adds Ella's longtime friend and musical colleague Benny Carter, "She has such an uncanny sense of hearing; she seems to hear every chord change there is. When she scats, she doesn't miss anything, and when she's singing something straight, it's pure."

While standing in the wings of a theater or a club, waiting to go on, Ella will almost always be nervous. She will follow her band out on stage by only a minute or two and usually unannounced. The audience will applaud all the longer because of the surprise of it. But her entrance echoes her personality: simple, straightforward, and unassuming. "I could do all the acting with a song, all the stuff with the hands and those gimmicks if someone showed me and I learned it. But it's not me," she once said.

After one or two opening numbers, she will pause to greet the house with a few simple sentences. "We'll sing some old ones, some new ones and some we don't even know!"

Then, colored handkerchief clasped tightly in hand to wipe away perspiration, and eyes closed to avoid annoying smoke, she will sing songs spanning every decade and every musical style and mood she has mastered during her long career. This could include Duke Ellington, Cole Porter, Burt Bacharach, Stevie Wonder; swing, bop, pop, Broadway; ballads and up-tempo pieces. On a ballad like "My Ship," her hand will cup her cheek just as her voice—dark, sensuous, comforting—caresses the melody. Off and running on "Take the A Train," she will keep time by slapping her hip with one hand. "Mountain

Greenery" might start out slow and stately, then become a runaway train, the beats punctuated by finger snapping.

If Ella is feeling particularly good, her snapping and slapping and swinging and swaying will turn into the old soft shoe, and Ella becomes the dancer of her childhood dreams. Just for fun, she might throw in a novelty number such as "Old MacDonald" and his "swinging farm" or pull out a harmonica. Always, she makes sure to include one or two crowd-pleasing scats. In these, Ella displays a voice with remarkable range and endurance and a remarkably sophisticated understanding of harmony and rhythm. As John Rockwell of the *New York Times* said, "She can not only hit whatever note she wishes, bending and coloring it at will, but she knows just the right note to select from the dizzying possibilities flying past her in the heat of a jazz improvisation." Writer Henry Pleasants says of her performances, "It is not so much what she does, or even the way she does it, as what she does not do. What she does not do, putting it as simply as possible, is anything wrong. There is simply nothing in her performance to which one would want to take exception. What she sings has the inevitability that is always a hallmark of great art."

Ella is famous for quoting other songs within a scat. In the middle of a bunch of unintelligible syllables in "Night in Tunisia," she might drop in a line or two from "A-Tisket, A-Tasket." The audience will laugh and applaud warmly in recognition.

At times, her voice will sound like a little girl's; at others, like a mature woman's, a trumpet, a trombone, a tenor saxophone, or even a growling Louis Armstrong.

In the early days if there was a heckler (there rarely has been since she's become a musical institution), she'd scold him by changing the words of whatever song she was singing into a warning. She's used the same technique to talk to the audience. After a particularly meandering improvisation on "St. Louis Blues," for instance, she has changed the words to "I guess these people wonder what I'm singing. Believe it or not, it's still 'St. Louis Blues.'"

If the concert is also going to feature some duets with a collaborator such as guitarist Joe Pass, the two might spend part of the intermission in her dressing room, picking out a set of tunes. But, Pass reports, "Once the two of us are onstage, anything can happen. I may surprise her by changing keys, even two or three times, but she'll be right on it, never missing."[2] Pass will usually open the second half of the concert with a few solo numbers. Then Ella will join him onstage and, with no other instruments to hide behind should something go wrong, the two will begin musically sparring, good friends challenging one another to greater musical heights with songs such as "Satin Doll," "A Foggy Day," and "I'm Beginning to See the Light."

After a few more numbers, Ella's backup trio will return for a short concluding set. To please younger audience members, Ella will usually try to include at least one popular song among them. Famed for her trouble in remembering lyrics, Ella will often read the words to an unfamiliar song from a sheet of paper. Ella created a big hit for herself when she first tried to sing "Mack the

Knife" without reading the lyrics. The audience screamed for her to sing the song, then popular in Germany where she was doing the concert, so she went along.

After singing three or four verses correctly, Ella sang, "What's the next chorus, To this song now, That's the one now, I don't know." But she plowed ahead anyway, making up her own lyrics as she went along, including one comparing herself to those who had already recorded the song.

"Bobby Darin and Louis Armstrong, Made a record, Oh but they did. And now Ella, And her fellas, Are making a wreck of, 'Mack the Knife'," she sang with her great good humor.

When it's all over, the audience will applaud loud and long. Even if she's not feeling well (as has often been the case in later years), and this was not her best performance, they applaud for all the other concerts, all the records, all the memories of the times her singing has brought them pleasure.

She acknowledges the applause with a humble, "Thank you very much, ladies and gentlemen. You've been a beautiful audience." She is also usually forced to return for an encore. After that, she will usually sing one or two more songs. Ella loves to sing. Never is that more obvious than when you see her in concert; after a few initial moments of nervousness, she will begin to smile and swing and just generally have a ball.

CHAPTER TWELVE

THE
HONORED
ELLA

In America in the mid-seventies, there was a revival of interest in jazz in general and Ella Fitzgerald in particular. Ella's songbook albums began selling in numbers not seen since they were first released. In September 1975, she, Frank Sinatra, and the Count Basie band got together for a twelve-day engagement at the Uris Theater in New York. The show grossed $1.08 million, the most ever earned by a Broadway attraction to that date. Ella also kept herself in front of millions by appearing on television shows and in commercials, at first for Memorex and later for American Express and Kentucky Fried Chicken.

The Memorex commercials, designed to show how well Memorex reproduces music, were especially popular and earned her six-figure fees. In the commercials, Ella sings a high note, causing vibrations that break a glass. Then a recording of her singing breaks another glass, and an announcer asks, "Is it live or is it Memorex?" After the commercials began airing, Ella endured a lot of good-natured kidding about her glass-breaking abilities. "On airplanes, sometimes the captain comes in and says, 'Don't you start singing because we don't want you to break the windows in the plane,' " she said. To children, she became "the Memorex lady." When Ella performed a concert for 13,000 of them in Columbia, South Carolina, and a television reporter asked one boy how he liked it, he said, "Well, I liked her singing all right but she didn't break no glass."

By the 1980s, Ella was performing about thirty-six weeks out of the year. It was the most demanding schedule she had attempted since her first eye problems, but it was more relaxed than the schedule she had maintained for most of her career. The first sign of other health problems came in August 1985, when she collapsed while doing a concert at Wolf Trap, just outside Washington, D.C. She was briefly admitted to a hospital for treatment of a fluid buildup in her lungs. A year later, the morning after performing a concert near Niagara Falls, New York, Ella began having trouble breathing while climbing the stairs at her hotel. She was admitted to a hospital, where doctors said they thought she was suffering from heat exhaustion. When newspapers printed the story, the hospital received 150 calls from concerned fans, including one from the White House. Back home in Los Angeles, Ella's own doctors put her through tests that showed that she had suffered a heart attack. In September 1986, she underwent a quintuple bypass operation on her heart and was given a pacemaker. After the operation, one of Ella's cousins, a minister, came to visit her and said, "You know, Ella, God performed a miracle on you." Said Ella, "When I found out afterward about the five-bypass operation, I knew he did."

Not long afterward, one of her toes was amputated because of poor circulation. These medical problems kept Ella at home for almost two years. To pass the time, she read, watched soap operas, knitted, and tried to get used to eating foods that were lower in fat, cholesterol, and salt. For years Ella had struggled with a weight problem, but after she began having heart problems she became thinner than she had been since she first began singing.

She also listened to records, discovering in the process some of her own that she had never heard before. "I used to think that people would think I was big-headed if I went into a record store and asked for my own records. So I never went," she explained. But now she could enjoy listening to them.

Perhaps Ella's greatest pleasure during her convalescence was visits from friends and family. Ella loves to entertain, and thinks nothing of inviting her whole family to her house for Sunday breakfast, or the entire Count Basie band in for a lasagna dinner. She especially looks forward to visits from her grandnephew and granddaughter. Ella's son, Ray Brown, Jr., lives with his wife and daughter in Anchorage, Alaska, where he is a singer-drummer in a country-western group. Ella had not met Ray Jr.'s wife before the marriage ceremony, and in 1983 said that she had yet to hear Ray Jr. sing professionally. She is probably closer to one of the nieces she helped raise who lives in greater Los Angeles. Being on the road so much of her life meant that she couldn't spend as much time with either of them as she would have liked.

"The main thing I missed was the children growing up, but all of them came out all right, thank goodness," she says. This one regret might explain her keen interest in children and charities for children. In 1976 she donated the proceeds from three nights of performances to help construct a child-care center that now bears her name in the Lynwood section of Los Angeles. Every Christmas, Ella gives the kids there presents. Says Ella, "If I were ever to do anything but music, it would have to be around children."

Nevertheless, not singing for almost two years was not easy for someone who had never had more than a few weeks' vacation at a time. When, in early 1987, her doctors said she could attend a rehearsal, Ella practically jumped out of bed to get there. "It felt so good. It gave me something to think about. I had spent so much time just lying with my legs up, wondering if I'd ever sing again." When she began performing again, now no more than a few times a month, she told her audiences that they were her best medicine. "I love what I do," she said. "It's the only thing, outside of children, I would want to do."

But the Ella Fitzgerald audiences were hearing in concert in the late eighties and early nineties was not the same singer they had heard a decade or two before. Some critics, such as Martin Williams, said Ella's voice had peaked in the mid-sixties and that it was never as good after that. Certainly by the 1980s, most agreed that her voice was now lower in tone, not as full and flexible, and occasionally, especially on long tones, impaired by a waver or scratch. Sometimes, when she was feeling especially unsteady, Ella performed while sitting on a stool. But she learned to compensate by sharing the stage with instrumentalists such as Joe Pass, by singing songs that showcased her sense of rhythm and vocal inventiveness and by putting more feeling into ballads than she had seemed capable of when younger. She once explained that in order to learn how to sing songs, "I had to experience different things, to learn how to tell songs like stories."[1] And yet, somehow, at the same time, her voice has retained the hope and innocence of her youth. "I'll always think of Ella as a young girl because she's never lost that wonderful quality," Frank Sinatra has said.

Grammy Awards that she won in 1984 and 1991 for the albums *The Best Is Yet to Come* and *All That Jazz,* respectively, are evidence of the continued excellence of her work. These pushed her Grammy total to thirteen, the most won by any female jazz singer.

In writing about her concerts during this period, reviewers noted her increasing ease onstage. Even John S. Wilson of the *New York Times,* a longtime critic of Ella's stage manner, noted how loose and relaxed she seemed in reviews of her concerts in 1979 and 1980. In a 1974 interview, she herself noted, "I'm doing more talking and I feel a little freer." One example was her reaction to falling onstage one night in Los Angeles in 1988. "Now people can really say Ella fell for them," she said into the microphone, while still in a prone position. Later, after resuming the concert, she sang a few bars of the Buddy Johnson song, "Since I Fell For You."

She had by this time also developed a more mature way of handling the conflicts with Norman Granz. "I used to pout a lot. Norman would holler at me and I'd cry, cry, cry all the time. It was making me very self-conscious. Now I'm at the point where I try to do the best that I can and beyond that I can't worry. And when I'm angry, instead of keeping it inside, I now speak my mind and then forget about it."[2]

She's also become better at accepting criticism. "I don't expect everybody to love my style of singing. For every one of those who don't like me there are those who like me." She's also "learned to have patience." Before, "Maybe I wanted things to happen too fast." But in later years, she learned, "Nothing good comes overnight. Just continue working, and [be] happy in what you are doing, and with God's will the rest will come."

Although Ella still grants interviews with reluctance, those who do talk with her find her to be sweet, unassuming, and straightforward. "It was like having a nice little visit with your grandmother," *Birmingham Post-Herald* reporter Kathy Kemp said of their interview.

It seems that in her later years Ella has been able to leave behind some of the insecurities that have plagued her for most of her life, although she still retains the humbleness her mother taught her the day she got cocky about starring in the school play.

"I always was taught that you're only as great as people make you. When you get to feeling that you know you're great, the heart goes out of things. I have to feel what I'm singing, and if I just walked out onstage and said, 'Here I am. Take me!,' it wouldn't be right," she has said.[3]

In 1990, colleague Benny Carter noted, "Certainly she's aware of [her fame], but she just takes it in stride, makes it look easy and feels so comfortable with it . . ."

If this is indeed the way Ella came to feel, it probably made it easier for her to enjoy the hundreds of honors and awards that have come her way since the late 1970s. Among the most important were ASCAP's Pied Piper Award; the Whitney Young Award of the Urban League, the community group that serves minorities; the Kennedy Center Honors in 1979, hosted by First Lady Rosalynn Carter; and the National Medal of the Arts, which she received from President Ronald Reagan at the White House in 1987. The last two awards were given for lifetime achievement in the performing arts. The Kennedy Center celebration was only the second time that these awards had been presented to performing artists. The other honorees included actor Henry Fonda, composer Aaron Copland, choreographer Martha Graham, and playwright Tennessee Williams.

In 1989, Ella was honored once again, this time by the Society of Singers in Los Angeles at a dinner where she received the first ever "Ella," an annual award named for her that will recognize America's greatest singers. The ceremony featured musical entertainment, a screening of some of Ella's movie and TV appearances, and dessert served in a yellow basket—in honor of "A-Tisket, A-Tasket." Proceeds from the party, which was hosted by Bill Cosby and attended by Los Angeles Mayor Tom Bradley and many Hollywood celebrities, were used for a fund to aid singers in professional or financial trouble.

Just a year later, another big fund-raising

party was held in New York City to honor Ella. Called Hearts for Ella, it included performances by such longtime friends and associates as Mel Tormé, Quincy Jones, Lena Horne, Benny Carter, Dizzy Gillespie, Bobby McFerrin, Cab Calloway, and Oscar Peterson, and, although she had not been scheduled to do anything but sit in the audience and enjoy the show, even a few songs by Ella. In recognition of Ella's heart problems, money from the benefit was used to establish an American Heart Association fellowship for doctors and scientists to study heart disease.

Presentations at these ceremonies and writings prompted by them talked about Ella's contributions to American society. Presenters at the Hearts for Ella gathering suggested that Ella's gift for improvisation has raised her impact beyond that of a mere song interpreter to the level of the country's greatest composers and instrumentalists. Commenting on her 1947 recording of "Lady Be Good," Benny Carter said, "I wouldn't call it 'Lady Be Good.' I would call it something like maybe 'Oh, Lady,' because that's what she sings: 'Oh lady, oh lady, oh lady be good to me.' When she goes into her improvisations on that record, everything she does following the opening chorus of that song is a composition."[4]

Singers ranging from Johnny Mathis to English soprano Dame Janet Baker have called her their favorite singer. Joe Williams, Pat Boone, and Lena Horne all said they grew up studying her records or wanting to sing like her. *Ebony* magazine has said that her uniquely adaptable talent has created a ". . . library of songs [that] constitutes as thorough a record as is available anywhere of America's changing moods and emotions."

According to John Rockwell of the *New York Times,* her style of singing actually blends "the major influences that have shaped American popular music in this century," making her a living history of that heritage. Radio personality Jonathan Schwartz noted that "the sound of her voice has been recorded more voluminously than the music made by any other single human being" with the sole exception of Bing Crosby. Leonard Feather said, "She is one of the elite for whom a single name on a marquee would suffice almost anywhere in the world." She is also, according to writer Henry Pleasants, one of the few who have been able to achieve wide popularity and esteem without compromising the qualities that endear her to fellow professionals and critics.

Many jazz singers have been critically acclaimed. Many pop singers have sold lots of records. But Ella has been able to have it both ways, for decades and decades. While many of those on the top of the record charts today are gone tomorrow, Ella's recordings continue to sell, to be played, to be used as themes for TV shows and movies. Her remarkable ability to adapt to different musical styles has not only kept people interested in her music, it's kept her interested as well. "You can get bored doing the same thing every night," she said. "I try to do a little of each. I love lyrics. I love ballads. But if I was to sing all ballads, I'd get bored." She's performed with symphony orchestras, big bands, trios or just one other musician. "Even if you do the same song with all these different settings it will give you the feeling of variety," she said.

Even those who lament Ella's lack of blues feeling, most notably Martin Williams, admit to being charmed by her exuberance, particularly noticeable on fast jazz tunes. Williams calls this "the stuff of joy." Echoed writer Colin MacInnes, "To hear her is to be given, in the most telling and pleasurable form, that particular lift of the spirits that is the gift of jazz . . ."

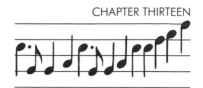

CHAPTER THIRTEEN

BACK WHERE IT ALL BEGAN

As someone who never finished high school, and has regretted it, Ella must be particularly pleased by the many honorary degrees she's received. They include degrees from Princeton, Harvard, Dartmouth, Boston University, the University of California at Los Angeles, Washington University, and the Peabody Conservatory. In 1982, Harvard's Hasty Pudding Club dubbed her Woman of the Year. After riding in a motorcade in an open car with ticker tape flying through the air, Ella arrived at a theater where students greeted her by singing "A-Tisket, A-Tasket."

When the University of Maryland dedicated the Ella Fitzgerald School of Performing Arts in 1974, the first time such a building was named for a black performer, Ella said, "Every night when I say my prayers I just thank God for the beautiful thing that happened to me and that I am here to see it. You know, so many things happen after people have passed, but here I'm seeing it. I just couldn't believe it."[1]

But perhaps none of these honors was as important as the degree she received from Yale University in 1986.

More than fifty years after Ella had tried out at a dance in one of the scientific colleges of that great university, a black girl from a ghetto with only a tenth grade education, Ella returned to be honored alongside Archbishop Cardinal Jaime Sin of Manila, South African novelist Nadine Gordimer, and ornithologist Roger Tory Peterson. As has often been the case in recent years, Ella was not feeling well on the day of the ceremony, so she leaned heavily on Yale Corporation Senior Fellow J. Richardson Dilworth as they paraded down the streets of New Haven in long academic robes before being seated on the graduation stage. It was a beautiful, sunny day.[2]

Ella noted, but did not comment on, the balloons some students carried that read "Yale Divest Now" to protest Yale's investment in stock of U.S. companies doing business in South Africa. Ella just folded her hands and waited quietly for her name to be called.

"Ella Fitzgerald, singer," Yale president, A. Bartlett Giamatti began as Dilworth helped Ella from her seat.

"Inspiration for vocalists and instrumentalists, your debut at a Yale Prom launched a career which has transformed American popular music into a sophisticated art known throughout the world. Your unique style and artistry are already part of the musical legacy of this century."

As Giamatti finished with the words, "Yale takes great pleasure in conferring upon you the

degree of Doctor of Music," the crowd of grad-
uates and their relatives stood and applauded.
People who had attended that university years
before had shown confidence in Ella's abilities,
and now they were thanking her for all the beautiful music she had brought the world since.

Source Notes

CHAPTER ONE

1. Henry Pleasants, *The Great American Popular Singers* (New York: Simon & Schuster, 1974), p. 175.
2. Quoted by Leonard Feather, "Ella: The Legend," *Los Angeles Times,* January 30, 1983.
3. Quoted in Barbarlee Diamonstein, *Open Secrets* (New York: Viking, 1972), p. 136.
4. Joel Siegel, "Ella at 65: 'A Lot to Be Grateful For,' " *Jazz Times,* November 1983.
5. Diamonstein, p. 135.
6. Ibid.

CHAPTER TWO

1. Quoted in Sid Colin, *Ella: The Life and Times of Ella Fitzgerald* (London: Elm Tree Books, 1987), p. 11.
2. Quoted in Arnold Shaw, *Black Popular Music in America* (New York: Schirmer Books, 1986), p. 139.
3. Quoted by Siegel.
4. Quoted in Leonard Feather, *From Satchmo to Miles* (New York: Stein & Day, 1971), p. 89.
5. Quoted in Colin, p. 22

CHAPTER THREE

1. Willie Ruff, in conversation with the author, Fall 1984.
2. Ralph E. Ellis, Jr., Yale Class of 1936, and Carleton Granbery, Jr., Yale Class of 1935, in conversation with the author, July 1991.

CHAPTER FOUR

1. Quoted in Feather, *From Satchmo to Miles,* p. 90.
2. Quoted in Colin, p. 47.
3. Bud Kliment, *Ella Fitzgerald* (New York: Chelsea House, 1988), p. 49.
4. Quoted in Kitty Grimes, *Jazz Voices* (London and New York: Quartet, 1983), p. 49.
5. Account of Webb's death in Barry Ulanov, *A History of Jazz in America* (New York: Viking Press, 1954), p. 173.
6. Quoted in Gene Fernett, *Swing Out: Great Negro Dance Bands* (Midland, Mich.: Pendell Publishing Co., 1970), p. 66.
7. Quoted in Kliment, p. 57.

CHAPTER FIVE

1. Quoted by Feather, *Los Angeles Times.*

CHAPTER SIX

1. Quoted in "Top Jazz Singer Tells How She Got That Way," *PM,* October 24, 1947.
2. Quoted in Dizzy Gillespie, *To Be, or Not . . . to Bop* (New York: Doubleday, 1979), p. 269
3. Ulanov, quoted in Pleasants, p. 177.
4. Gillespie, p. 273

CHAPTER SEVEN

1. Quoted by Leonard Feather, "Ella Today (And Yesterday Too)," *Down Beat,* November 18, 1965, p. 22.
2. Quoted by Siegel.
3. Quoted in Gillespie, p. 408–9.
4. Quoted by Siegel.
5. Quoted by L. Robinson, "First Lady of Jazz," *Ebony,* November 1961, p. 138.
6. Quoted in ibid., p. 137.
7. Quoted in Colin, p. 121.
8. Quoted in Feather, *From Satchmo to Miles,* p. 93.

CHAPTER EIGHT

1. Quoted by Feather, *Down Beat,* p. 22.
2. Quoted in the *New York Post,* May 4, 1958.

CHAPTER NINE

1. Quoted by Robinson, p. 137.
2. Quoted in Leslie Gourse, *Louis' Children: American Jazz Singers,* (New York: Morrow, 1984), p. 259.

CHAPTER TEN

1. Quoted by Feather, *Down Beat,* p. 22.
2. Quoted by Leonard Feather in "Ella Fitzgerald: Lonely at the Top," *New York Post,* October 17, 1965, p. 56.
3. Quoted in Colin, p. 124.
4. Quoted by Feather, *Los Angeles Times.*
5. Quoted in Grimes, p. 49.

CHAPTER ELEVEN

1. Quoted by Ernest Dunbar in "Ella Still Sings Just This Side of the Angels," *New York Times,* November 24, 1974.
2. Quoted by Leonard Feather in "L.A. Honors the First Lady of Song," *Los Angeles Times,* April 23, 1989.
3. Quoted by Robinson, p. 136.

CHAPTER TWELVE

1. Quoted by Siegel, *Jazz Times.*
2. Quoted by ibid.
3. Quoted by ibid.
4. Quoted in *Newsday,* April 25, 1990.

CHAPTER THIRTEEN

1. Quoted by Dunbar, p. 15.
2. J. Richardson Dilworth, in conversation with the author, August 1991.

Selected
Discography

The Best of Ella Fitzgerald. Volumes 1 and 2. (MCA cassette 4047-E and 4016-E) Singing on the Decca label from 1938 to the early 1950s.
1935–40. (L'Art Vocal CD 5, and Classics CDs 500, 506, 518, 525 and 566) Series of 6 recordings, identified only by years, spotlight her work with Chick Webb and her own short-lived big band.
Ella Sings Gershwin. (MCA cassette C-215E) Solo piano accompaniment by Ellis Larkins.
Lady Be Good! (Verve cassette 825 098-4) Ella as she sounded with the Jazz at the Philharmonic group.
The Irving Berlin Songbook. Volumes 1 and 2. (Verve LP 829 533-1; cassette 829 533-4; CDs 829 533-4 and 829 535-2). Winner of Ella's first Grammy Award.
The Duke Ellington Songbook. (Verve LP 827 163-1; cassettes 829 163-4 and 827 169-4; CD 837 035-2). Another Grammy winner. Contains Ellington's tribute, "Portrait of Ella Fitzgerald."
The George and Ira Gershwin Songbook. (Verve LP 825

024-1; cassette 825 024-4; CD 825 024-2) Considered by many to be Ella's best.

The Harold Arlen Songbook. Volumes 1 and 2. (Verve LP 817 526-1; cassette 817 526-2; CDs 817 527-2 and 817 528-2). Billy May arranged these songs by one of the most jazz-influenced of popular composers.

Mack the Knife: Ella in Berlin. (Verve LP 825 670-1; cassette 825 670-4; CD 825 670-2) Some say Ella is never better than when performing before a live audience. Includes her first performance of her famous scat hit, "Mack the Knife." Also a Grammy winner.

Fitzgerald and Pass: Again. (Pablo cassette 52310-772; CD 2310 772-2) Grammy winner. Work with a longtime guitarist colleague.

Ella & Louis. (Verve cassette 827 176-4; CD 825 373-2) Not showing Ella in her best light, but important for showcasing two jazz legends together.

A Perfect Match. (Pablo Today LP 2312 110; cassette 52312 110; CD2312 110-2) Grammy winner showcasing work with longtime collaborator Count Basie.

Ella Wishes You A Swinging Christmas. (Verve LP 827 150-1; cassette 827 150-4; CD 827 150-2) The swingingest Christmas album ever.

Ella in Rome: The Birthday Concert. (Verve LP 835 454-1; cassette 835 454-4; CD 835 454-2) Live concert recorded on Ella's birthday in 1958.

The Best is Yet to Come. (Pablo Today LP 2312 138; CD 2312 138-2) Grammy winner.

All That Jazz. (Pablo LP 2310 938; cassette 52310 938; CD 2310-938-2) Grammy-winning example of Ella's most recent work.

Bibliography

Anderson, Jervis. *This Was Harlem: A Cultural Portrait 1900–50.* New York: Farrar, Straus and Giroux, 1982.

Cerulli, Dom; Korall, Burt; and Nasatir, Mort. *The Jazz Word.* New York: Ballantine Books, 1960.

Colin, Sid. *Ella: The Life and Times of Ella Fitzgerald.* London: Elm Tree Books, 1986.

Crow, Bill. *Jazz Anecdotes.* New York and Oxford: Oxford University Press, 1990.

Dahl, Linda. *Stormy Weather: The Music and Lives of a Century of Jazzwomen.* New York: Pantheon, 1984.

Dance, Stanley. *The World of Swing.* New York: Scribners', 1974.

Diamonstein, Barbarlee. *Open Secrets.* New York: Viking Press, 1972.

Dunbar, Ernest. "Ella Still Sings This Side of the Angels." *New York Times:* 24 November 1974.

Feather, Leonard. *From Satchmo to Miles.* New York: Stein & Day, 1971.

————"L.A. Honors the First Lady of Song." *Los Angeles Times Calendar:* 23 April 1989, p. 4.

————"Ella Today (And Yesterday Too)." *Down Beat,* 18 November, 1965.

————"Ella: The Legend." *Los Angeles Times Calendar:* 30 January 1983, p. 1.

Fernett, Gene. *Swing Out: Great Negro Dance Bands.* Midland, Mich.: Pendell Publishing Co., 1970.

Fox, Ted. *Showtime at the Apollo.* New York: Holt, Rinehart & Winston, 1983.

Gillespie, Dizzy. *To Be, or Not . . . to Bop.* New York: Doubleday, 1979.

Gourse, Leslie. *Louis' Children: American Jazz Singers.* New York: Morrow, 1984.

Green, Benny. "The Ella Fitzgerald/Norman Granz Songbooks: Locus Classicus of American Song." *High Fidelity,* March 1980.

Grimes, Kitty. *Jazz Voices.* London and New York: Quartet, 1983.

Harrington, Richard. "In the Key of Ella: At 70, the Fabulous Fitzgerald is Still Setting the Standards." *The Washington Post:* 6 May 1988.

Haskins, James. *Black Music in America: A History Through Its People.* New York: Crowell, 1987.

Kliment, Bud. *Ella Fitzgerald.* New York: Chelsea House, 1988.

Morgenstern, Dan. *Jazz People.* New York: Abrams, 1976.

Osofsky, Gilbert. *Harlem: The Making of a Ghetto; Negro New York 1890–1930.* New York: Harper & Row, 1966.

Pleasants, Henry. *The Great American Popular Singers.* New York: Simon & Schuster, 1974.

Robinson, L. "First Lady of Jazz." *Ebony,* November 1961.

Rockwell, John. "Half a Century of Song with the Great Ella." *New York Times:* 15 June 1986.

Schiffman, Jack. *Harlem Heyday.* New York: Prometheus Books, 1984.

Schwartz, Jonathan. "Ella: She's Brought us Fifty Years of Exquisite Music. . . ." *Esquire,* November 1985.

Shaw, Arnold. *Black Popular Music in America.* New York: Schirmer Books, 1986.

Siegel, Joel. "Ella at 65: 'A Lot to Be Grateful For.' " *Jazz Times,* November 1983.

Simon, George T. *The Big Bands.* New York: Schirmer Books, 1981.

———*The Best of the Music Makers.* New York: Doubleday, 1979.

———*Simon Says: The Sights and Sounds of the Swing Era.* New York: Galahad Books, 1971.

Ulanov, Barry. *A History of Jazz in America.* New York: Viking Press, 1954.

Williams, Martin. *Jazz Heritage.* New York and Oxford: Oxford University Press, 1985.

Index